ARISE

NIGERIA

GLEANING HOPE FROM THE NIGERIAN STORY

PETER OVIE AKUS

DEDICATION

I dedicate this book to my Creator who blessed me with the gift of writing.

TABLE OF CONTENTS

ACKNOWLEDGEMENT

I am profoundly grateful and eternally indebted to everyone who has played one role or the other in making this book a reality.

ARISE NIGERIA

PREFACE

The 1999 presidential elections in Nigeria held on the 27th of February 1999. The Independent National Electoral Commission (INEC), the body that oversees electoral matters in the country, registered only three political parties for the elections. They were the People's Democratic Party (PDP), the All People's Party (APP) and the Alliance for Democracy (AD). This was an improvement to the two party system that the military had run in the 1993 elections.

As the nation proceeded to the election grounds, one man stood against INEC and insisted that three parties could not represent a nation of about 150 million people. That man was Chief Gani Fawehinmi. Gani Fawehinmi was a lawyer and a human rights advocate. He was known to have engaged in many battles with authoritarian and repressive military dictatorships, in times past, on behalf of the ordinary people of Nigeria. He argued that Nigeria, having recovered from military rule, should have a lot more political parties available to them to choose from.

So immediately after the 1999 elections, Gani Fawehinmi entered into a protracted legal battle with INEC. When the case was not decided in his favour in the lower courts, he took it to the Supreme Court of the nation. On November 8th, 2002, the Supreme Court read its judgement that stated in part:

> *"INEC had no power to make guidelines on how an association can become a political party so far as the Constitution has covered the field in section 222... to restrict the formation of political parties weakens the democratic culture...[1]"*

The Supreme Court granted Gani's prayers that INEC should register more than just three parties for elections in Nigeria. In the buildup to the 2003 general elections, therefore, INEC was compelled to register 27 more parties; bringing the total number of parties in the country's

---

[1] Ossai, Aaron. 2018. 'Wike and Proliferation of Political Parties'. Pressreader. 16th February, 2018. Accessed: 2nd December, 2019.
www.pressreader.com/nigeria/thisday/201802216/281526521526396

electoral system to 30. In the 2019 election, 68 parties had been registered by INEC. The proliferation of political parties in the nation's electoral system is the product of one man's battle for the expansion of the political space through the judicial system. This story of Gani Fawehinmi is a miniature picture of the Nigerian story itself.

Arise Nigeria tells the Nigerian story over an approximate 200 year period. Nigeria, like most other countries in the world, was created based upon power play by the European powers. Nigeria came into being when the Europeans came to this land with the hope of harnessing resources from it to fuel their bludgeoning industrial revolution. While slave trade had been largely abolished in the British Isles, Europeans still needed raw materials for their industries and the production lines that were coming out of them.

When the Europeans arrived in Africa and Nigeria, in particular, they realized that they must organize the largely scattered nation states that they met on ground into a unit. In the process, they introduced a central government which they manned and protected with a virile army. Using mind manipulations, and in many cases force, the Europeans took over much of the lands belonging to the Nigerian people. But a combination of doggedness, a growing class of educated Nigerians, and the fact that colonialism was fast losing fashion in the eyes of the whole world, made the Europeans relinquish power to Nigerians. This picture of a people recognizing what they want and pursuing it, like it was depicted in the Gani Fawehinmi case, would replay itself not only in the days of the Europeans but even when a Northern oligarchy sought to rule the nation exclusively – the country revolted. This, unfortunately, resulted in a thirty month fratricidal war that ended in 1970.

By the close of the war, Nigerians came face to face with a new hegemony. It was no longer the Europeans or a Northern oligarchy; this time it was the military. Yet, the Nigerian people held up their stance: Nigeria sought for democratic rule and not the governing of its people by a set of men holding the reins of a rifle. After a lot of ups and downs, the country entered into a period of sustained democracy from 1999 up till this moment.

Arise Nigeria traces the Nigerian story. I have chosen to write this book with a perspective of hope to the Nigerian story. While the Nigerian story is usually told in doldrums, I have chosen to glean hope from the situation in this country. Some of the things that we would see play out in the Nigerian story is the efforts of ordinary Nigerians calling for an independent Nigerian state. And even after that was granted, Nigerians still sought a nation that was rid from autocratic rule.

One of the least told story of an emerging Nigeria is the efforts of the Nigerian Press to see this country emerge from the grips of those who had chosen to use her for their own pecuniary gain. Whether it was during the time of the British, or the time when one ethnic group sought dominance over others; or the time when the military held sway, the Nigerian people always knew what they wanted and they pursued it.

It is 105 years after the amalgamation of Northern and Southern Nigeria. It is also almost 60 years since this country gained independence from British rule. The usual narration by most Nigerians is that the country is not moving forward. Some Nigerians tend to speak of the "good old days". But the records speak otherwise. Nigeria has made a lot of progress since its amalgamation and independence. It is difficult to appreciate this progress except one takes the time to weigh them.

The religious song says to "…count your blessings one by one and you would see what the Lord has done…" *Arise Nigeria* is a record of God's blessings on a single country. While at the same time narrating the challenges, I have sought to extract hope from the pages of our history. I do wish that those who would read this book will find it enlightening and challenging enough to pursue a Nigeria that we all would be proud of in the days to come.

What is clear to all who have followed the Nigerian story is this: if this country will get better every Nigerian would have to be committed to the rule of law. And a commitment to the rule of law does not only begin in the courts but first with a people who are determined to keep the laws of the country in the privacy of their homes and to encourage others to do the same. Then we must have a proper policing system that would enforce the keeping of the rule of law. The Nigerian Police Force is overdue for an overhaul. With a proper policing system in place, then we can be sure that there is a strong and effective agency of government to enforce court rulings.

While a proliferation of parties in Nigeria's electoral system has become some sort of an impediment for INEC today, the fact that citizens can resort to a higher and unbiased power to fight for their rights is evidence of a nation state that is moving forward. Chief Gani Fawehinmi's story is just one out of many other stories in Nigeria's history. Arise Nigeria will be telling a lot more of these stories with an eye to show that while Nigeria is not where she wishes to be today, she is a lot farther from where she started from.

Peter Ovie Akus.
January, 2020

ARISE NIGERIA

CHAPTER ONE

COLONIAL NIGERIA AND THE AMALGAMATION

On the 19th of December, 1852, a girl was born to Captain George Shaw and Marie Adrienne Josephine. Her birth took place at 2, Dundas Terrace, Woolwich, in South London. As it is the custom with the British, the baby girl was named at birth; she was given the name Flora – perhaps to accentuate the beauty of a flower radiant on the girl child's face as she cried out searching for nourishment like every healthy child would.

Flora Shaw grew up in an upper middle class family. Her father, George Shaw, would later rise to become a Major General in the British army. Flora had a happy childhood, growing in the midst of her thirteen other siblings – two of whom died in infancy.

Flora Shaw was born at a time when the industrial revolution had reached its peak in England. The country had two major issues facing it at that time. First was the astronomical wealth coming to it through her increased production of goods that were being sought for not only in Europe but also in the United States of America. Then there was the trouble of having to find raw materials to feed these production needs.

Britain had abolished Slave Trade and she was championing its abolishment in other parts of the world; so the only other option to find material for the huge production line that England faced was to search out the newly found territories of Africa. Already, British expedition had sailed for the black man's continent and news reaching producers about the discovery of raw materials in Africa were quite cheering. Flora Shaw grew up in a Britain that had jettisoned one evil – Slave Trade – to take up another evil – Western Imperialism.

Following her tertiary education, Ms. Shaw took up a career in writing. From 1878 to 1886, Shaw had written five novels. All of them were written for children and young adults. Her first book, **Castle Blair**, became quite popular in the United Kingdom and the United States. It was a book based on her childhood experience. Ms. Shaw would eventually take up a career in journalism in 1886.

She wrote for the Pall Mall Gazette, Manchester Guardian, and The Times of London. On the 8th of January, 1897, Ms. Shaw wrote an article titled "Letter" where she suggested "Nigeria" to the British Government as the name that should be given to the area around the Niger, in the lower part of the Sahara. This was a territory of Africa the British people had very keen interest in because of its proximity to the sea and its abundance of natural resources. Shaw wrote further:

> *"The name Nigeria applying to no other part of Africa may without offence to any neighbors be accepted as coextensive with the territories over which the Royal Niger Company has extended British influence, and may serve to differentiate them equally from the colonies of Lagos and the Niger Protectorate on the coast and from the French territories of the Upper Niger[2]"*.

At the time of writing this article, Flora Shaw was also the mistress of a British military officer, Sir Frederick Luggard. Also, at about this time, Britain was bringing finishing plans to taking over the administration of the region that would later be known as Nigeria from a company called the Royal Niger Company. This company had been pushing British interest in Nigeria before this time. But on January 1st, 1900, Britain took over the running of Nigeria from this company. Sir Fredreick Luggard became the High Commissioner of the newly created

---

[2] Shaw, Flora. (8th January, 1897). *"Letter"*. The Time of London. Page 6

Protectorate of Northern Nigeria at this time. He and Ms. Shaw, who was six years older than him, were married on the 10th of June, 1902. Ms. Shaw was now known as Lady Luggard. All of these events sum up to make, what had first begun as a mere suggestion in 1897 in a newspaper publication, a reality in the naming of a country. Lady Luggard's close relation with men of power and means, would eventually influence the naming of the soon to be the greatest black nation on earth – the country called Nigeria.

The Beginning

Henry the Navigator (1394-1460) was the fourth son of a King of Portugal. Prince Henry had developed a passion for travels and explorations. He is today known as the main initiator of the Age of Discovery. The Age of Discovery is a period in the 15th and 16th century when Europeans developed a strong desire to explore the world to map out new trade routes with other continents.

Europeans were particularly interested in reaching Asia, where the large populations of the Chinese and Indians offered new business opportunities. With the leadership of Prince Henry, the Portuguese soon developed a reputation for being explorers. In their explorations, they discovered the continent of Africa and were greatly enamored by her size, weather, and natural resources. Africa Today gives this account of Portuguese coming to Nigeria:

> *"The Portuguese were the first Europeans to reach the site of modern Lagos, in 1470; they visited Benin in 1472 and in 1486 the King of Benin exchanged ambassadors with the King of Portugal.[3]"*

Following the coming of the Portuguese to Africa, other Europeans began to come to Africa to seek out business opportunities. These Europeans would eventually buy into the greed of many African chiefs to perpetuate the capturing of black Africans who were subsequently sold as slaves to European countries. The white man discovered quite

---

[3] Africa Today... Page 1163*

early that the use of slaves on his farm was a cheap source of labor that came with much productivity and subsequently great wealth.

In a short while, from the fifteenth to the eighteenth century, Slave Trade became big business. The coastal area, south of the Sahara desert, quickly came to be known as the Slave Coast. However, with the abolishing of Slave Trade by the British Parliament in 1833, Slave Trade would eventually experience a decline. It would be abolished in 1865 when the United States of America brought an end to the evil.

While the British ended the purchasing and selling of slaves, they would eventually return to Africa to purchase raw materials for the booming and rapidly expanding industrial revolution that hit Britain and the whole of Europe in the early part of the 19th century.

The British appointed John Beecroft as Consul of the Bights of Benin and Biafra in 1849 to essentially regulate trading in Benin, Brass, Calabar, Bonny, Bimbia and the Cameroons. In a very short time, Beecroft had clashed with King Kosoko of Lagos, who resented Britain's interference with his lucrative business of Slave Trading. The British eventually deposed Kosoko and installed his nephew, King Akitoye, as King of Lagos in 1852.

King Akitoye died in December 1853 and was succeeded by his eldest son, Prince Dosunmu. The British would again return and pressurized King Dosunmu to sign a treaty ceding Lagos to the British. In 1862, Lagos was declared a British colony. The name "Lagos" itself was given to the area around the coast by the Portuguese. It described a land that was surrounded by "lakes". This act opened up the islands around Lagos and other parts of Nigeria to business opportunities for British firms to come to Nigeria to purchase raw material for industries in Europe.

In 1879, four of the largest British firms doing business around the coast of Lagos and in other parts of Nigeria, came together and formed a single company called the United African Company. They did this to end competition among themselves and to constitute a united front against other competing forces from Europe, particularly companies from France. With this united front, the UAC, again changing its name to National African Company (NAC), sought to have treaties with various local rulers within Nigeria. These treaties were hastily done. An example of such a treaty said that the Nigerian parties:

> *"... fully recognized the benefit accorded to our country and people by our intercourse with the National African Company Limited, and in recognition of this we now cede the whole of our territory to the NAC, and their administrators, forever.[4]"*

Such was the simplicity with which the British defrauded Nigerians.

In 1886 the NAC changed her name to the Royal Niger Company Chartered and Limited. In the same year the Berlin Conference was inaugurated. The Berlin Conference essentially partitioned Africa among the various competing European nations that had come to the African soil to get raw material for the ongoing industrial revolution in their land. At the conference, the British made a firm claim for the two regions that is today known as Nigeria and the Cameroons.

The Royal Niger Company (RNC) would immediately move into full gear to administer the region around the Niger (now known as Nigeria). The RNC appointed Sir George Goldie as political administrator over the land, with his headquarters in Asaba. Goldie spent the next decade trying to quell resistance and insurrection by the locals who resented the obvious colonization of their land by the British.

To aid British economic interest in Nigeria, the British Parliament sent a military man, Captain Fredrerick Lugard, to the country. In March 1898, Lugard arrived with a troop of 2,000 men and quickly silenced the resistance in the land. His unit was called the Royal West African Frontier Force. It was the first military unit in Nigeria and the Nigerian military bore this name up till 1960 when the nation gained independence from British rule[5]. On December 31, 1899, the British government revoked the charter of the Royal Niger Company and assumed ruling of Nigeria on January 1st, 1900. Thus began the sixty year colonization of Nigeria.

---

[4] Africa Today... 1164

[5] Yesufu, Deji. Victor Banjo.... Page 5.

Northern and Southern Protectorate

While the British brought both western culture and religion to bear on the southern parts of Nigeria, the north of Nigeria remained largely uninfluenced by the British culture. For ease of governance, the British divided Nigeria into two: the Northern Protectorate and the Southern Protectorate in 1900. The Southern Protectorate was separate from the colony of Lagos. The colony of Lagos only became part of the Southern Protectorate in 1906.

The Northern Protectorate or what we now know as Northern Nigeria was a nation that was steeped in the Islamic religion and traditions. This had come about as a result of the work and influence of a man called Usman Dan Fodio (1754-1817). Shehu Usman Dan Fodio was born in Gobir town (in present day Sokoto State). 'Dan Fodio was a Fulani who had been brought up in the Islamic religion. He soon became a much listened to teacher of Islamic law and began to gather a following in the town of Gobir.

His criticism of the local rulers' over taxing the people led to a near attempt on his life in 1802. 'Dan Fodio fled Gobir but would return in 1804, with a group of men, to take over the town from those who were perceived to be oppressing the people. He called his war a jihad. By 1808, 'Dan Fodio's Jihad had taken over the northern towns of Kano, Daura, Katsina, Zaria, Gombe, Nupe, Adamawa and up to the fringes of Borno. It was only the Borno emirate he could not conquer.

So that by his death in 1817, the influence of 'Dan Fodio religion had pervaded the whole of what we now know as northern Nigeria. 'Dan Fodio was succeeded by his able and charismatic son, Muhammed Bello, who continued to spread the influence of his father's campaign. The seat of Usman dan Fodio's power is the Sokoto Caliphate, which remains the most powerful monarch in northern Nigeria till today.

It was this deeply Islamic influenced culture that the British met in 1900 when they began to rule northern Nigeria. Britain made Sir Frederick Luggard the first High Commissioner to the Northern Protectorate in 1900. Luggard brought in a system of indirect rule to Northern Nigeria. It meant that the British colonialists would not be having direct dealing with the locals; rather they would be ruling the land through their emirs and chiefs. Luggard also brought forward a system of governance that allowed the people of the North to practice their religion and culture with little or no influence of Western education.

Luggard actively opposed the activities of European missionaries in Northern Nigeria and discouraged the preaching of the gospel in north. The result was that northern Nigeria was not exposed to Western culture and it also meant that very little Western education reached the North in those days. While in one hand, it won Luggard a lot of favor with the local Hausa rulers; on the other hand it set northern Nigeria back. So that by the time the Southern part of the country was well educated and ready to lead the nation at independence, the North had very few educated elites.

The Southern Protectorate of Nigeria was formed in 1900 and its first High Commissioner was Ralph Moore. In 1906, Lagos colony was added to the Southern Protectorate. So that this region ran all the way from after the River Niger down to Lagos in the South; while at the same time stretching to as far as the Niger Delta area of the country.

The Southern Protectorate or the south of Nigeria, unlike the North, was already exposed to Western culture and Christianity by the time of its birth. A lot of Nigerians had already begun to see the advantage of having their children get Western education. Even by this time, Nigerian elites were already sending their children to schools in Britain to acquire Western education. These young people came back with bright ideas to help impact their country for good. It was not long before these young men and women began to clamor for the independence of Nigeria from colonial rule.

The Amalgamation

In the decade following 1900, Britain became weighed down with economic challenges and the prospect of the coming crisis that eventually culminated in the First World War that started in 1918. Thus the leading discussion at the time was how to cut down the cost of administering the various colonial outposts of the British all around the world and this would include the two regions in Nigeria.

It was therefore not difficult for the colonial powers to reach the conclusion that the cost of running one region in a country would be less than the cost of running two regions. Thus, based solely on economic reason, and ignoring the vast cultural and religious differences between the North and South of Nigeria, Britain reached the conclusion to bring together the two regions of Nigeria. This coming together was called *"amalgamation"*.

The word had not been used anywhere else in the world as a political action; it was used for the first and the last time in Nigeria. Lord Luggard took office as Governor of both the Southern and Northern Protectorate in 1912 and quickly set in motions machineries to ensure the coming together of the two parts of the country. The Northern and Southern Protectorate were eventually brought together in the Amalgamation exercise of 1914. Lord Luggard became the first governor of the newly created territory.

A lot of people have argued against this amalgamation process. Osuala and Muoh, writing in a paper titled *"The Doldrums of Nigeria's Amalgamation"*, stated:

> *"To the northern zone is the predominance of the Hausa/Fulani and Kanuri extraction. The South is dominated by two competing ethic groups: the proud and culturally rich Yoruba people whose cradle of civilization had been attributed to Ile-Ife in south-west and the energetic, industrious and vibrant Igbo in the south-east. Hemmed in between them were approximately over two-hundred and fifty disparate ethnicities with over three-hundred and fifty languages. Among these are the Efik, Ibibio, Jukun, Nupe, Tiv, Idoma, Edo Ijaw, Itshekiri, Igbira, Illaje, etc. thus, the region was a multiplicity of groups with divergent political, economic, cultural, religious, as well as philosophical worldviews. It is these distinct groups that the colonial administrators merged in 1914.[6]"*

Osuala and Muoh went on to argue in their paper that putting such disparate number of ethnic group together in such a hasty manner was unwise and thus the reason why the unity of the nation is being greatly threatened today. This led them to making this important point that:

> *"The more than fifty geo-political entities known today as 'African Countries' were the arbitrary creation of European imperial powers in the course of the so-called 'scramble for Africa'. In these creations, territorial boundaries were demarcated with no regard to the cultural differences of the various nationalities that occupy these territories. In some cases, coherent cultural groups were split by different border lines; in other cases, distinct, or even rival groups, were brought together to form a single colonial entity. No doubt, the absence of an 'organic' cultural or 'national' identity which is a common denominator of most modern political entities in the Western world is lacking in Africa. There is a broad consensus among scholars on the artificiality of Africa's current political boundaries. These scholars all emphasize the effects of the process of boundary creation during that era of colonialism on the career of the post-colonial African state.[7]"*

Like Osuala and Muoh, most African intellectuals hold the view that the amalgamation of Nigeria, that also led the British to bring many other such distinct entities in other African countries together, was a mistake. This has led to the dismembering of many such countries. The Rwandan genocide of 1994 was blamed on the Belgian colonialists who, in a similar hurried manner, put the Hutu and Tutsi tribes together.

The government of Paul Kegame has succeeded in keeping Rwanda together by simply abolishing the whole idea of ethnicity in the

---

[6] Osuala U. S. and Muoh U. O. 2015. 'The Doldrums of Nigeria's Amalgamation: A Historical Re-Appraisal'. Research on Humanities and Social Sciences.(ISSN 2225-0408). Page 80
[7] Ibid. Page 79

country. Today, in Rwanda, it is a crime to claim to be either Tutsi or Hutu. Countries like Sudan were however not that lucky. After years of political wrangling over the inappropriateness of their being together, a referendum was held and South Sudan voted to pull out of Sudan. Despite having achieved this separation, South Sudan is still embroiled in a civil war over who controls the country's rich supply of crude oil.

Providence

Nigerians have the choice set before them: we may either live with what has been bestowed on us by our colonialists or we set out a new path for ourselves as a nation. What we should however note is that separation may not necessary mean achieving successful nationhood as we have seen in the example of South Sudan. We may however choose to follow the example of Rwanda who chose to make a success of their disparity.

It is the humble position of this writer that a lot more was involved in the making of Nigeria than the factors that has been enumerated in this chapter. It is a fact that every nation can trace its beginning to one factor or the other. For Nigeria, it only happened that a brilliant female journalist, Flora Shaw, was the one Providence ordained to name the country. Besides, all that she did was to give a name to an already existing entity. Africa, despite being largely an uncivilized territory in the 18th/19th century, could not avoid joining the movement towards civilization like the rest of the world. In the 19th century when the Europeans came to govern Africa, they met a system of loosely connected towns and peoples.

The world had gone beyond that and the Europeans quite naturally formed us into a body polity of nation states. This, again, one considers to be the working of Providence. It is untrue that if Nigeria were to divide into ethnic nation states, we would run well. The fact of the matter is that the moment division begins, there usually is no end to such divisions. Most ethnic groups that claim brotherhood today will eventually turn on each other as they separate into smaller units. The testimony of countries like South Sudan, Somalia and the former Yugoslavia is that even communities that speak the same language and trace their roots to the same stock, can still be enmeshed in sustained warfare and civil strife.

Nigerians can accept our history of being colonized and the 1914 amalgamation as the workings of Providence. We can make this nation work because there is are lot of advantages in diversity. We can employ the vast array of land in northern Nigeria and work it into a sustainable agricultural edifice that can feed Africa and supply the rest of the world with raw materials for industry.

We can also take the vastly educated Yoruba of Western Nigeria to cooperate with the industrious and commerce oriented Igbos in Eastern Nigeria to build a nation that the League of Nations can envy. We can better channel the proceeds of oil that is coming from the Niger Delta and use it to develop this country. As we proceed at discovering the hopes enmeshed in the history of Nigeria, we as a people can develop a new perspective to building a great and developed nation state. We can see the amalgamation and our being colonized as a blessing and not a curse.

CHAPTER TWO

INDEPENDENCE AND SUBSEQUENT CRISIS

The challenge of having disparate kinds of people and groups come into nationhood has been a foundational trouble with Nigeria. The British who created the concept of a modern Nigeria state brought different regions of the nation together solely for their own advantage. So that by the time Nigeria began to develop into nationhood, bringing these different groups of people into one nation, would remain a daunting task for our founding fathers. It was Chief Obafemi Awolowo that wrote:

> *"Nigeria is not a nation. It is a mere geographical expression. There are no 'Nigerians' in the same sense as there are 'English' or 'Welsh' or 'French' – the word Nigeria is merely a distinctive appellation to distinguish those who live within the boundaries of Nigeria from those who do not.*[8]*"*

On another occasion, the first Prime Minister of Nigeria, Sir Abubakar Tafawa Balewa, was quoted as saying:

> *"... since the amalgamation of Southern and Northern*

---

[8] Awolowo, Obafemi. *Path to Nigerian Freedom.* (London. Faber and Faber. 1947). Page 47-48.

> *provinces in 1914, Nigeria has existed as one country only on paper, it is still far from united. Nigerian unity is only a British intention for the country.[9]"*

These two statements are a picture of the challenge that the founding fathers were facing when the new nation state called Nigeria was created. It would not be far-fetched to claim that it still remains a challenge for us today.

Problems Following the Amalgamation

After the amalgamation of the Northern and the Southern Protectorate in 1914, Sir Frederick Lugard brought the system of indirect rule that he had utilized in the Northern Protectorate, while he was Governor there, as the system of governing the whole country. While indirect rule may have worked in the North, because the people were already being ruled by the Usman Dan Fodio emirate system of governance, and all the British needed to do was to rule the people through their already recognized leaders; it failed to work in Southern Nigeria because there were no such centralized systems of governance there.

For example in Eastern Nigeria, where there were no central rulers at all, the British created something called ***"Warrant Chiefs"***. The Warrant Chiefs then ruled Eastern towns and villages on behalf of the British, while at the same time reporting to the colonial masters. The Igbo man, who originally sees himself as lord of both his home and environment, detested the idea of another man dictating to him what he must do.

This resorted in many protests against taxation laws and other laws imposed on the people by the British. The most popular of these protests is the Aba Women riot of 1929/30, where thousands of women took to the streets, protesting the British tax assessment drive that was rumored to include the taxation of women and children.

A similar challenge was experienced by the British in Western Nigeria, even though the people there were already used to some kind of some

---

[9] Balewa, Tafawa. Quoted in *Hansard*. (Lagos Government Printer. 1947.)

kind of central government by the Yoruba Obas. However, prior to the coming of the British indirect rule, the Obas were not sole authorities in the strict sense; neither did they collect taxes from the people. Yoruba land had always practiced some kind of democracy even before the coming of the British. Before long, the people revolted against the British. Examples of this would include the Iseyin-Okeho riots of 1916 and the Egba revolts of 1918.

In addition to these, the amalgamation, rather than unite the country, further accentuated its distinctiveness. Lugard appointed two Lieutenant-Governors to oversee both the Northern and Southern Protectorate. Lugard himself stayed in Lagos from where he coordinated the two regions. This system of governance discouraged the integration of the two regions, besides the other matters of differences they already possessed and these distinctiveness were further worsened as the country neared independence.

Lord Lugard would remain in control of Nigeria until 1918 when he retired. His book, *"The Dual Mandate in British Tropical Africa"*, published in 1922, is an important documentation of the history of colonial administration in Africa.

Agitations for Self Rule

Southern Nigeria had an advantage that the North did not have. It had the presence of Christian missionaries. Lord Lugard had discouraged the activities of missionaries in the North, so that most of their missions was situated in the South of the country. The Christian missionaries possessed a different vision from the colonial masters. Even though they were both Europeans, and sometimes Americans, these missionaries had something more than the pursuit of economic gain in their activities.

They sought to preach the gospel and help the locals gain understanding of the kingdom of God. They discovered quickly that the easiest way to do this was through education. Therefore the missionaries encouraged a lot of the indigenous people to send their children to the numerous schools that the churches were forming in those days. Before long, quite a number of Nigerians had possessed Western education. Equipped with an education and understanding the dynamics of society and governance, many of these young men and women began to clamor for self-rule. Here is a picture of the agitation in those days:

> *"Nigerians in Lagos began to agitate for a measure of participation in the existing government structure. The colonial government thereafter responded with a semblance of participatory government. The process led to the establishing of the Nigerian Council (in 1914), which comprised of 24 officials and 12 unofficial members. The body, which was essentially advisory, had no legislative powers. Six of these unofficial members were Europeans representing commercial, shipping, mining, and banking interests, while the other six were Africans. The African comprised the Sultan of Sokoto, the Alaafin of Oyo, the Emir of Kano, Chief Douglas Numa and two educated Nigerians representing Lagos and Calabar, respectively[10]..."*

Nigerians had at this time moved from being mere spectators in governance to at least participating in government at "advisory" level. In 1922 the first Nigerian political party was formed by Sir Herbert Macaulay. Macaulay was a Surveyor and the party he formed was called the Nigerian National Democratic Party (NNDP). The party's leading manifesto was for Nigeria to achieve self-government within the British Empire. On March 29th, 1934 another political party was formed by Dr. J. C. Vaughan.

He was a medical doctor and he named the party the Lagos Youth Movement. It would later become the Nigerian Youth Movement (NYM). On the 26th of August, 1944, the Nigerian Union of Students in Lagos formed a party called National Council of Nigeria and the Cameroons (NCNC) and Herbert Macaulay was elected as its first president. In 1946, when Herbert Macaulay died, Nnamdi Azikwe, a

---

[10] Nigeria's Golden Book. *The Problems of Amalgamation.* (The Sun Publishing Limited. Lagos, Nigeria. 2010.) Page 48.

journalist, who was formerly the general secretary of the party, became President of the NCNC.

As political groups were being formed in the South of Nigeria, some elites in the North also began to form political groups. In May 1948, the Jamiyar Mutanen Arewa (Union of the People of the North) was formed. Its founding members were Dr. R.A.B Dikko and Sir Ahmadu Bello. This group would metamorphose into a political group called the Northern People's Congress (NPC) in 1951.

A break-away group from this political party, led by Aminu Kano, would go on to form the Northern Elements Progressive Unions (NEPU). On March 21st, 1951, Chief Obafemi Awolowo announced the formation of the Action Group (AG) at his house in Ibadan.

All of these parties would become the active political forces that would wrestle political power out of the hands of the British. But, as it would have been noticed, their formations were clearly along ethnic and regional lines. So that while the British had accentuated the disparity in the Nigerian nation with its creation of a Northern and Southern Protectorate, Nigeria's foremost politicians worsened the divide by creating political parties that appealed mostly to regional sentiments.

The Making of Nigeria's Constitutions Pre-Independence

As the clamor for self-governance continued to increase all around the country, the British saw the need for the making of a constitution that will explain in detail the mode of governance in Nigeria. Within this constitution, Nigerians could then seek elective office and be directly involved in the governance of their own country for the first time.

In 1922, Sir Hugh Clifford, the Governor General of Nigeria, who had succeeded Lugard, led the formation of a constitution which is today known as the Clifford Constitution. This constitution created a legislative house for Lagos and the Southern Provinces. The legislative house had a number of Nigerians elected. This was the first time Nigerians would be involved in governing their own people.

In 1946, the Clifford Constitution was replaced with the Richard's Constitution. It was named after Sir Arthur Richard the Governor of Nigeria at the time. This Constitution created a central legislative body that could oversee the whole country for the first time. It was also this constitution that divided the country into North, West and East. The Constitution sought to promote unity in Nigeria and that is why it created a central legislative arm for the whole country.

In 1948, when Sir John Macpherson became Governor of Nigeria, he also proposed that there should be constitutional amendments. He made this proposal because there were endless criticism of the Clifford Constitution and Macpherson felt that some of the criticisms were valid. The Macpherson constitution was then brought forth in January 1950. This constitution provided for both a central and regional system of government.

It meant that there were going to be central legislators to oversee the whole country in the country's House of Representatives and regional legislators to oversee the three distinct regions of the country. This constitution also provided modalities for the proposed general elections for the whole country that was slated for 1951. Quite expectedly, when Election Day arrived in 1951, the NPC gained control of the Northern House of Assembly. The AG controlled the West and the NCNC controlled the East.

In 1954, another constitution was created for the country by the various politicians from the three regions of the country. This constitution was called the Lyttleton Constitution. This constitution detached Lagos from the Western part of the country and made it a Federal territory. It also detached Southern Cameroon from Eastern Nigeria.

This constitution empowered each region of the country to make its own laws, although the Federal government still retained powers over all regions and could intervene in any region in times of crisis. The constitution made allowance for each region to be led by "Premiers", while the whole country was to be presided over by a Governor-General; with the Prime Minister being over the House of Representatives.

When the Lyttleton Constitution came into force on the 1st of October 1954, Ahmadu Bello of the NPC became Premier of Northern Nigeria. Obafemi Awolowo of the AG became Premier of Western Nigeria; and Nnamdi Azikwe of the NCNC became Premier of Eastern Nigeria. The Lyttleton Constitution made Nigeria into a federation.

Independence on October 1st, 1960

Another conference was held in London from May 23 to June 6, 1957 to examine the question of self-government. The Eastern and Western Regions of Nigeria requested for self-government during this conference. These two regions would become self-governing on August 8th, 1957. Northern Region did not become self-governing until March 15th, 1959. This conference agreed to increase members of the House of Representatives, the central legislative arm of the country, to 320. It also agreed to create the office of a Prime Minister for the country.

The Prime Minister would have powers to appoint ministers he can work with, following recommendations to the Governor-General of the country. It was at this conference that the Nigerian delegation make a united demand for independence from the British government. Prior to this time, most of the agitation for independence had come from the Southern Regions, while the North was pussy-footing. But a united demanded for independence was difficult for the British to resist. Besides this, many countries in the British Commonwealth had become to enjoy self-governance.

The following African countries had gained independence from the British even before Nigeria: Egypt (1922), Libya (1951), Sudan (1956), Ghana (1957), and Somalia (July 1st, 1960). So the clamor for self-rule was quite universal in Africa, Britain was reeling from the debt of having fought two world wars in a row, and they were quite willing to let go off the colonial grip they had over Nigeria.

On September 2, 1957, Alhaji Abubakar Tafawa Balewa was appointed Nigeria's first Prime Minister. He was serving under the Governor-General Sir James Robertson. Balewa would immediately form a government that included six ministers from the NCNC, four from the NPC, two from the AG, and one from the Cameroon National Congress (KNC). He did this to show the British that Nigerians could govern themselves in a coalition of parties.

A final pre-independence constitutional conference was held in London from September to October of 1958. This conference agreed that Nigeria would become independent on October 1st, 1960. Elections were to be held around the country in December 1959. These elections to the House of Representative led to the NPC winning all the 148 seats in the North; the NCNC-NEPU alliance won 89 seats; and the AG alliance with the United Middle Belt Congress (UMBC) won 75 seats.

The NPC and the NCNC entered into a coalition which kept Balewa as Prime Minister and the head of the government in Parliament, while Dr. Nnamdi Azikwe was to become Governor-General of the newly independent country. Azikwe would resign his office as Premier of the Eastern Region, while Dr. Michael Opara succeeded him. Chief Obafemi Awolowo left his office as Premier of the Western Region to become leader of the opposition in the House of Representatives. Alhaji Ahmadu Bello, though leader of the NPC, chose to remain as Premier of Northern Nigeria and delegated his deputy, Balewa, to go to Lagos and lead the new government.

These are the political scenarios when Nigeria gained independence from the British on October 1st, 1960. On the outside there was a lot of joy and celebrations by the people of the country. On the inside, however, the political machinations that shored up the new government in Nigeria was soon going to become extremely heated up, leading to an implosion in the country that just could not be avoided.

Crisis Following Independence

The beginning of the crisis in the newly independent Nigeria started when a number of Nigerians felt that the best minds were not given the opportunity to lead the new nation. It was quite clear to all that Northern Nigeria was not as erudite as their Southern counterpart. The

North had delayed entering self-government largely because they did not have enough indigenous people to run their civil service.

They were greatly dependent on the British and other Nigerians from the Southern parts of the country to run their government for them. In fact Nigeria's independence had delayed that long because the North was not ready for self-rule. Therefore not a few persons were pleasantly surprised when the leadership of the country was given to the North. Deji Yesufu writes about the British influence on those who eventually governed Nigeria at independence:

> *"The British gave Nigeria the parliamentary system of government. Each region of the country had a number of representation at the Federal Parliament and each region had its regional parliament too. The number of seats allocated to a region at the Federal Parliament was dependent on the population of that region. Through their Tripartition Act, the British attributed a greater population figure to Northern Nigeria than the South. They did this because they desire that the North would rule the country. This desire was borne out of a malicious position against many southern agitators for independence, for it was common knowledge in those times that Northern Nigeria would have preferred that the British held the reins of government until a later time. The British therefore rewarded them handsomely for their submissiveness.[11]"*

The 142 seats that the NPC got at the House of Representatives, as against the 89 for the NCNC and the 75 for the AG, came largely from this Trapitition Act of the British. Southern Nigeria, which was more enlightened than the North, could still have come to power if the NCNC and AG had agreed to power sharing.

But Nnamdi Azikwe and Obafemi Awolowo could not agree on the mode of sharing power. Azikwe would eventually give in to the offer

---

[11] Yesufu, Deji. *Victor Banjo.* (Joe-Tolalu & Associates. Ibadan, Nigeria. 2018) Page 11.

by the NPC and took the NCNC into alliance with the people from the North. Thus the new country was birth in an atmosphere of mutual mistrust, intrigues and personal vendetta.

The first sign of trouble for the fledgling country appeared when Nigeria held her first census in March 1961. The matter of the appropriate number of people in the country was important because this is what would determine the number of seats each region shall have in the House of Representatives. The initial count in this census revealed that Northern Nigeria did not have the population that the British census, conducted before their exit, had.

When the NPC government realized the implication of this, they canceled the census exercise and scheduled another for 1963. The census of 1963 was allegedly doctored to favor the numbers that the North desired. Although the AG was not in power, Obafemi Awolowo and other members of his parties in parliament were giving the Balewa government a lot of trouble.

Awolowo was the publisher of the Tribune newspapers and thus there were no short supplies of editorial comments in that paper that embarrassed the Balewa government. The NPC decided to invade Awolowo's party and create a division among them. Ahmadu Bello, a master of intrigue, reached out to Chief Samuel Ladoke Akintola, the Premier of the Western Region at the time. When the AG realized that Akintola was hobnobbing with the government at the center, he was brought to trial for anti-party activities.

He was found guilty and asked to resign his office as Premier. When he would not resign, the Western Region House of Parliament empowered the Governor of the Region, Oba Adesoji Aderemi, to remove Akintola from office. Adesoji deposed Akintola but Akintola would not relinquish power. All of these began to happen in 1962.

The crisis in the Western government would soon spill out of control, mandating the central government of the NPC to step in. A state of emergency was imposed on the Western Region and Akintola was forced to step down from office. In his place, Dr. Moses Majekodunmi led the new administration in the Western Region.

The Majekodunmi administration instituted a panel to investigate the crisis and Akintola was found not guilty. The Balewa government would promptly install Akintola back to office in December 1962. The AG appealed the case to the British Privy Council – the body that acted as the nation's Supreme Court in those days. The British Privy Council ruled in favor of the AG but the Balewa government refused to obey the courts. This was part of the reason why the Balewa government sought to make Nigeria a republic in 1963 and wholly cut off ties with the British.

The NPC, led by Tafawa Balewa, would proceed to charge Obafemi Awolowo, leader of the opposition in Parliament, and ten others, with charges of treasonable felony on September 1963. They were tried in court and found guilty under Justice Sowemimo – who had said during the trial that his "hands were tied", indicating a clear interference in the judicial procedure by powers from above. Awolowo and ten others were found guilty and imprisoned.

In 1964 the country went to the polls to elect their leaders. Parties that were loyal to the Balewa government swept the polls clean both in the North and in the Western region. The people of the West, who clearly did not vote for Akintola's party, the Nigeria's National Democratic Party (NNDP), became incensed and plunged the whole Western region into a crisis. Politicians were killed and properties were burnt. The newly independent nation was tethering to self-destruct.

Education

This chapter has looked at the events that led to Nigeria gaining independence from the British. We have traced the factors that added up to making it difficult for the British to remain as colonial leaders. One point that we may take away from these events is this: the Nigeria people were able to achieve independence from colonial masters not by force of arms but through an enlightened mind. The Nigeria people gained independence through education.

By the turn of the 20th century, Nigerians were already returning to the country with tertiary education. The Anglican Bishop, Samuel Ajayi

Crowther, by the 1840s, had already began to publish books. He would eventually publish a translation of the Bible into the Yoruba language. Thus there was a rich heritage of educated Nigerians even when the British arrived to colonize Nigeria in 1900. In addition to these, the Western Government of Chief Obafemi Awolowo, when it came to power in 1955, immediately made education free for all children from primary to secondary school level.

This singular action would lead to the educating of a mass of Nigerians of the Yoruba stock, so that by the 1970s, Yorubas became the intellectual capital of the country. And up till today, the people from Western Nigeria remain the leading thinkers in the country. Their contribution to national discourses in books and the news media, including the recently founded social media, has often been the basis through which public opinion has mounted pressure on the government to effect policies that would favor the common people.

The challenge that we are however facing with pursuing education in our time however is not that people do not know the advantage that education could bring to them; it is that many Nigerians see education as a means of deliverance from economic deprivation only. In fact right from colonial days, Nigerians had begun to see that those who possessed an education were those who were useful to the white men; they were the ones who earned more in the civil services and so on.

So the tendency was for economically disadvantaged people to get their children and wards educated so that they could get jobs and so that the whole extended family unit may be delivered from penury. Today, in 21st century Nigeria, the story is fast changing. Possessing an education is not a guarantee to get a job. Nigerians are therefore beginning to see the proper place of the mind being enlightened.

Education will liberate the mind and thus cause the human being to seek for the liberation of others all around him. Gradually, we are beginning to realize that education should not be pursued for personal gain alone; we should seek to get educated so that we may bring good to the collective. The education that men like Obafemi Awolowo sought to instill on the Western Region was such that brought social development to all and not just to one person or to his family unit alone.

Therefore the take-away from this chapter must be that an investment in the education of a people is an investment in the future development of those people. While education is an expensive venture, every government that has a long term development agenda for its people must be committed to investing in it. Education would liberate the minds of people and this would subsequently lead to their liberation from every ill that may be besetting them.

In the first half of the century in Nigeria, colonialism was the ill besetting the Nigerian nation and it was education that led the way to the people finding their freedom. It is also through education that the dividing lines of religions and tribalism can be erased in the Nigerian state. As people become more and more enlightened, we will realize that our collective humanity is more of a binding force than religion and ethnicity. It is only enlightened minds, through sound education, that can reach this height of thinking and behavior.

CHAPTER THREE

COUPS

Major Patrick Chukwuma "Kaduna" Nzeogwu was not feeling very well at midnight of 15th January, 1966. He was suffering from a flu, obviously from being overly exposed to the elements because of the midnight training he and his men had been undergoing in the past two weeks near the road leading to Zaria from Kaduna town. Tonight was "H-Hour" and Nzeogwu was not in the mood to allow a mere catarrh get in his way.

He had driven himself to the point where he was to meet with the other revolutionaries. This was some five miles from the well secured home of the Sardauna of Sokoto. When he arrived, his leading revolutionaries where already present. Major Timothy Onwuatuegwu and Captain Ben Gbulie were standing with a group of well-trained men who had been selected for this operation. Nzeogwu spoke:

> *"Officers and soldiers, welcome to Operation Damisa... As we all know, Damisa is the Hausa word for the leopard; an animal that is known to never change its spots. This is a perfect description of our corrupt politicians who are a symbol of filthiness through bribery, corruption and nepotism. They are not ready to change and if we can't change them through the ballot, we shall, by God, change them through the bullets.[12]"*

---

[12] Akinbode, Ayomide. *A Carnage Before Dawn* (Okadabooks. Nigeria. 2017)

With those words, Nzeogwu proceeds to reiterate their plans. Major Timothy was to proceed to the home of Brigadier Ademulegun and effect his arrest. Ademulegun was the GOC of the Kaduna army division and the revolution would not succeed if he was not arrested. Captain Gbulie was assigned to arrest another senior officer: Colonel Shodeinde. Shodiende was a senior officer and his arrest was crucial also. The plan was clear: if these men resisted arrest, they were to be neutralized. With those words the men jumped into their vehicles, while the soldiers assigned to assist them followed them in trucks.

Nzeogwu and his men proceeded to the home of the Sardauna of Sokoto. It was about 2am and they appeared to still be on track as far as time was concerned. The Sardauna of Sokoto, Alhaji Ahmadu Bello, was the Premier of Northern Nigeria and arguably the most powerful politician Nigeria has ever had. Ahmadu Bello had just returned from Hajj and was hoping to spend the weekend with his family before resuming work on Monday.

He did not know that fate had other plans for him. Nzeogwu and his men drove to about a kilometer of the Sardauna's house and then switched off the lights on their vehicle. The guards at the gate of the home of the Premier were police officers. Nzeogwu and his men promptly arrested them and cuffed them.

The soldiers then proceeded to bring out the 84mm Carl Gustav anti-tank recoilless Rifle. It was a weapon that was used mostly to stop the extremely destructive military tanks on their tracks. Nzeogwu and his men planned to use it to blow open the Sardauna's impregnable gate. Having set up the Gustav, Nzeogwu gave orders to fire. The first shot brought the gates down. This was followed by a volley of gunshots from the mutinous soldiers. They continued to shoot for about five minutes. When Nzeogwu saw that the house was already burning, he ordered that firing should stop. He then led three other men into the building while the others waited outside to keep watch.

As they approached the building, Nzeogwu could see members of the Sardauna's home running around in panic. It suited him well, as such confusion was needed to hatch his plan. He was about to take a turn into the main building, when a man in flowing white gown appeared suddenly with a dagger and slashed Nzeogwu in the arm. He was aiming for his head but was not that lucky. The men following their boss promptly dispatched the man to the great beyond. This man was one of the Sardauna's bodyguards. A bandage was quickly wrapped around Nzeogwu's arm and he proceeded to the main quarters.

Nzeogwu and his men ransacked every room in the house. While they saw some women and children, the Sardauna was nowhere to be found. They kept shouting, "Where is the Premier?" But there were no coherent answers. The soldiers understood that they needed to find the Premier themselves. Just as they were despairing of finding him, Kaduna noticed a rather large gathering of women and children in a particular room. They were all hovered on a spot. He moved towards these people and again demanded for the Premier.

No one spoke. He then dragged the oldest woman out and threatened to shoot. It was at this point that Ahmadu Bello emerged from where he was hiding among the women and children. Nzeogwu commanded him to step aside from the people. He obeyed but his eldest wife, Hafsatu Bello, ran towards the Sardauna and demanded that if Nzeogwu would kill her husband, he would have to kill her first. Nzeogwu simply said: "Have your wish…" He opened fire and immediately killed her and her husband.

Mission Accomplished

Nzeogwu called out to his men and they drove to the army barracks. He would later be informed that Shodeinde and Ademulegun had resisted arrest and had both been killed. He was particularly unhappy that Ademulegun's pregnant wife was also killed but Onwuatuegwu made it clear that it could not be avoided. By 5am of 15th, January, 1966, the coup that will forever change the history of Nigeria had been completed. By the time Nigerians were waking up to their business that Saturday morning, the news of the coup had already been announced on the radio.

The June 29th, 1966 Countercoup

By the time the dust of the violence of the January 15th, 1966 coup will settle, the following leading politicians had been killed: Prime Minister

Tafawa Balewa, Premier Ahmadu Bello, Premier Samuel Ladoke Akintola, and Finance Minister Festus Okotie-Eboh. Save for Bello, the others were killed in Lagos; while Akintola was killed in Ibadan. Leading officers that were consumed with the revolution will also include Brig. Samuel Ademulegun, Brig. Zakariya Maimalari, Col. Ralph Shodiende, Col. Kur Mohammed, Lt. Col. Abogo Largema, Lt. Col. James Pam, and Lt. Col. Arthur Unegbe.

The leaders of the coup were Major Chukwuma Nzeogwu, Major Ifeanyi Ifeajuna and Major Adewale Ademoyega. Nzeogwu had carried out the coup in the North successfully and was holding the reins of power in that region of the country. The putsch failed in Southern Nigeria because the mutinous soldiers could not lay their hands on the most senior officer in the army then, Maj. Gen. Aguiyi-Ironsi.

So, while Nzeogwu was announcing the take-over of government on the radio in the morning of January 15th in Northern Nigeria, in the South of the country Ironsi was in hiding. Lt. Col Yakubu Gowon and other senior officers swung into action and in a short time, the revolution was arrested in Lagos. The revolution had hardly kicked off in the East before the soldiers assigned to arrest Michael Opara and other politicians there were arrested by soldiers loyal to Aguiyi-Ironsi. In three days, all the soldiers involved in the coup had been arrested and slammed in jail.

Maj. Gen. Aguiyi-Ironsi agreed to form a government of military officers, after his colleagues in the army had recommended that they lead the country. Prior to January 15th, 1966, Nigeria had never known military rule. So there was a lot of novelty that needed to be dealt with. Ironsi got all the mutinous soldiers locked up in prisons all around the country. He however must have stepped on the shoes of Northern officers and soldiers by doing this.

Some of these soldiers felt that given the magnitude of blood that followed the coup, the soldiers involved in the January 15th coup ought to have been court-martialed and if found guilty, executed. For reasons best known to Ironsi, he did not do this. Instead he sought to stabilize the country politically. Ironsi instituted a decree that gave the central government that he was heading more powers than any central government in Nigeria had had before that time.

He was also accused of unduly promoting soldiers of Eastern extraction above their colleagues from other regions of the country. The idea that "the Igbos were now in power" became a nuance that pervaded most of public life and Northerners, who had hitherto enjoyed this privilege, did not like this. The atmosphere for a counter-coup was already in the making.

On the night of July 28th, 1966, a group of Igbo officers and soldiers had gathered at the Abeokuta barracks to discuss national issues. Word got around that these officers were gathering to plan a coup that would exterminate all Hausa soldiers in the Nigerian army. As the meeting progressed, suddenly Northern soldiers bust into the meeting and opened fire on all the Igbo officers present in that meeting. Everyone was killed.

That same night, Ironsi was on a state visit to Ibadan. He was guest of Lt. Col. Adekunle Fajuyi. He had completed the ceremony for the day and had retired into his quarters when things went out of hand. At about midnight, Lt. Col. Yakubu Gowon put a call to Major Theophilus Danjuma, who was the head of the security for the Commander, Aguiyi-Ironsi. Gowon informed Danjuma of the killings in Abeokuta and requested that whatever happens, the Head of State must be kept alive.

Danjuma made it clear he would ensure his safety. The discussion between this two carried the notion that there was indeed a need to take power from Ironsi, but that Ironsi's life was to be spared. The nation could not afford another round of bloodbath. Danjuma got into his military fatigue and headed to the room of the Commander. He entered Ironsi's room and announced that he had come to arrest him. Ironsi immediately understood the situation. He requested to wear something warm and then join Danjuma. On their way out, Lt. Col. Adekunle Fajuyi intercepted them and protested Ironsi's arrest.

He said Ironsi was his guest and if he would be arrested, they would have to take him also. Therefore Danjuma cuffed the two of them. Danjuma, would however state in a newspaper interview[13] that when he stepped outside the guest house that night with Ironsi and Fajuyi, the

---

[13] PM News Nigeria. How I Arrested Ironsi – Theophilus Danjuma. 1st October, 2019. www.pmnewsnigeria.com...how-i-arrested-ironsi-theophilus-danjuma

whole place had been taken over by Northern soldiers who were demanding for Ironsi's blood. Before he could take charge of the situation, he was pushed aside.

The soldiers took Ironsi and Fajuyi to the outskirts of Ibadan where they were both beaten to death. It is worth noting that by the end of the July 29th coup, no less than 200 officers and soldiers of Eastern extraction had been killed.

For the next two days, the country degenerated into pandemonium. Igbos in the North were summarily killed by Hausas. Many of them were slaughtered en-masse as they sought to return to the East. Igbos in Western Nigeria were not spared either. This situation would later force the Governor of the Eastern Region, Col. Emeka Ojukwu, to declare that he could not guarantee the safety of Igbos anywhere outside the Eastern Region. He called on his people to return home. This call precipitated a mass exodus of Igbos to Eastern Nigeria.

Lt. Col. Yakubu Gowon was appointed to lead the new military government. Gowon and Ojukwu could not agree on many issues concerning the political situation in the country. Ojukwu blamed Gowon for sitting still while Igbos were being murdered all around Nigeria. He threatened Gowon with secession. Gowon warned Ojukwu not to even try it. On the 27th of May, 1967, after months of brick-batting between the two military leaders, the Nigerian government, headed by Gowon, divided the Eastern region into three state.

They did this to whittle down Ojukwu's powers. The former Eastern region then gave rise to Rivers State, Cross River State, and the East Central State. The East Central State is the present site of Imo, Enugu, Abia, Anambra and Ebonyi States. The Gowon government ensured that the state Ojukwu ruled over, the East Central State, was land-locked; while he gave independent status to minority groups in the Eastern parts of the country. Three days later, Ojukwu announced that the Eastern Region had seceded from Nigeria. Gowon therefore announced police action on the first week of June.

The Nigeria civil war had effectively started. The war would rage on for thirty months, coming to an end on January 8th, 1970. Ojukwu fled the country, while Gowon and others took over the running of the whole country. The civil war came to an end officially on the 12th of January, 1970, when Major General Effiong, the man who succeeded Ojukwu as commander of the Biafran army, signed the documents at Dodan Barracks, Lagos, saying that Biafra as a nation had ceased to exist.

The Muritala Mohammed Coup

On October 1st, 1970, General Gowon, the head of the Nigerian government, announced that the Supreme Military Council (SMC), handing over power to a civilian government on January 1st, 1976. But before that would happen, Gowon explained further, there was a need to bring about proper reconciliation among Nigerians and reconstruction of areas of the country that had been mostly affected by the war. He called this "a nine point agenda" and pledged government's commitment to it.

To address the foundational course of the Nigerian civil war, Gowon instituted a census in the country on November 25th, 1973. The census figures put Nigeria at approximately 80 million people; with the Northern parts of the country having 51 million and the Southern parts having a population of 29 million. These figures were greatly disputed among Nigerians. Some people claimed that Nigeria was the only country in the world were the population of the people tended to decrease as the country approached the sea.

A situation that was naturally not practical since it is a foregone conclusion among population experts that people tend to make their habitation around coastal areas. The Gowon government was also accused of corruption. Nigeria had just come into new found wealth with the coming of the Oil Boom. Gowon was quoted as saying that Nigeria's problem was not money but how to spend it. Unfortunately, much of the country's wealth was being frittered away via corruption.

The straw that would break the camel's for the Gowon's administration was when he announced at the nation's independence celebrations in 1974 that the January 1976 date for a return to civilian rule was no longer feasible. This announcement sparked a great deal of protest from the Nigerian populace but there was even more disaffection among the rank and file of the military.

It was a known secret in the military that sometimes after the civil war, Gowon and Brigadier Muritala Muhammed had fallen out. Muritala accused Gowon of high handedness and laxity in handling the growing corruption among the elites in the Nigeria government. Gowon felt that Muritala was insubordinate but he could not remove him from the army because of his popularity among a high number of Northerners in the military.

Muhammed and a few other officers had instigated the July 29th, 1966 coup that removed Ironsi from office and they had agreed to put Gowon in power because he was the most senior officer among them. Muritala was therefore known to boast openly that the same way he and others put Gowon in power, they would also remove him. When Gowon announced that there would not be a return to civil rule, Muritala saw the unpopular move by the government as an opportunity to remove his principal from office.

On July 29, 1975, General Gowon was away to Kampala, Uganda, for an Organization of African Union conference. While there, Brigadier Muritala Ramat Muhammed announced a takeover of government. He accused Gowon's government of being "characterized by lack of consultation, indecision, indiscipline, and even neglect"[14]. Muritala was declared the Head of State of Nigeria. Gowon was informed of his removal from office in the middle of one of the sessions at the OAU. He quickly excused himself to find out more details. Gowon never returned to Nigeria. He fled to the United Kingdom and used his time there to further his education.

Muritala's first action in government was to cancel the disputed census results of 1973. He also announced his government commitment to return power to civilians on October 1, 1979. Muritala immediately moved to purge the nation of corruption. In the exercise that followed, some 10,000 civil servants were retired from service. Another one 1,000 officers and soldiers in the military were retired.

Muritala instituted the creation of more states in Nigeria, bringing the number of states in the country from 12 to 19. On February 3, 1976, Muritala announced that the government had finalized plans for a creation of Federal Territory at the heart of the nation, which would be

---

[14] Africa Today... Page 1173

called Abuja. The Muritala government is seen by many today as one that was committed to bettering the lot of Nigerians. It was Afrocentric and dynamic.

The Dimka Coup

On the morning of Friday, 13th February, 1976, General Muritala Muhammed was being driven to work. In the car were his driver, orderly and his aide-de-camp (ADC). Muritala had disposed of the usual security paraphernalia that many Heads of States were known to bandy around. There were no escort around him except for the vehicle he was driving in. He also lived in his official quarters in Ikoyi, Lagos.

His car had stopped at a traffic light and they were awaiting being passed, when gunmen, dressed in flowing civilian gowns, opened fire on his vehicle. The car, a Peugeot 504, was riddled with bullets. It is believed that the Head of State was killed almost immediately. The man who led the onslaught on Muritala that day was Lt. Col. Buka Suka Dimka. The Dimka coup, would eventually be foiled.

Further investigations into why the coup was carried out revealed that a section of army officers from the Middle Belt of the nation, particularly the Plateau area, were not happy with the way and manner Gowon had been removed from power. They therefore sought to remove Muritala and install Gowon back as Head of State of the country. An army panel of enquiry was instituted and in all 31 military men and one civilian were found guilty of having plotted the assassination of the Head of State.

They were all sentenced to death by firing squad. Some top army officers killed along with Dimka include Maj. Gen. I. D Bissala and Lt. Col. J. D. Gomwalk. Gowon was also accused of having instigated the coup. But Gowon gave a statement from his base in Britain that he had no hand in the coup. The Nigerian government sought his extradition to Nigeria to answer to charges levied against him but the British government refused to send him back to Nigeria.

Lt. Gen. Olusegun Obasanjo succeeded Muritala as Head of State. He had been deputy to Muritala until the latter was assassinated. Obasanjo is quoted as saying of Muritala death:

> *"... for me personally, this has been one of the saddest moments of my life... we all mourn the passing away of one of the greatest sons of Nigeria... I have worked very closely with him and I have shared his beliefs and commitment to the Federal Government's policies and actions. I believe and feel strongly committed to all that we have been doing. I pay him no better tribute than to continue the spirit with which he handled this country – that of complete dedication.[15]"*

Obasanjo and the Supreme Military Council (SMC) under him continued Muritala's commitment to return power to civilians in 1979. Obasanjo therefore oversaw the transition program that saw the emergence of Alhaji Shehu Shagari as the President of Nigeria in October 1st, 1979.

The Buhari/Idiagbon Coup

The second republic began on the 1st of October, 1979, with Alhaji Shehu Shagari as President. He had emerged the presidential flag bearer of the National Party of Nigeria (NPN). His closest rival at the polls was Chief Obafemi Awolowo of the Unity Party of Nigeria (UPN). Shagari's emergence as President became disputed when his opponents alleged that he did not win two-third majority of the 19 states of the federation, as the electoral laws required.

Two-thirds of 19 would have been twelve two-third. Yet, Shagari won only 12 states of the federation. The Supreme Court would however uphold Shagari as winner of the 1979 election and he was sworn in. The events around Shagari's coming to power would however continue to cause widespread acrimony between political parties – about the same situation that greeted the new Nigerian state in 1960.

The Shagari government also did not help matters because it was alleged to have been brazenly corrupt. While Shagari himself was not

---

[15] Africa Today... page 1174

known to be corrupt, members of his cabinet were said to have continually enriched themselves while the President looked on helplessly. One such individual in Shagari's cabinet was his Minister for Transport, Umaru Dikko. Max Siollun writes of Dikko:

> *"... Dikko... was the ultimate personification of 1980s corruption and shady deals in Nigeria. Stories of his alleged corruption are legion. As well as being Transport Minister, Dikko headed a notorious presidential task force set up to alleviate food shortages by distributing imported rice. The task force was accused of hoarding rice in order to artificially exacerbate existing food shortages and drive prices even higher. It was also accused of issuing import licenses to businessmen with connections to the ruling NPN. Dikko's name became synonymous with corruption..."[16]*

Besides Dikko, other members of the Shagari government were also accused of corruption. What however caused the greatest uproar against the Shagari government was their handling of the 1983 general elections. The elections had been hotly contested, with the NPN and the UPN as leading contenders.

Shagari had returned unopposed as the flag bearer for the NPN; while Chief Obafemi Awolowo was the flag bearer of the UPN. The results of the elections were strongly disputed and this afforded the military the opportunity to return to power. One of the army officers that led the removal from office of Shagari, Ibrahim Babangida, is quoted as saying:

> *"... We could have toppled that government in 1982, before the (1983) elections. But then, we said no, because the people would be against us. We knew damn well that they were not going to conduct that elections freely and fairly, and, therefore, we waited for the right time. You see, to stage a coup, there is one basic element that everybody looks for; there must be frustration in the society...[17]"*

---

[16] Siollun, Max. *Soldiers of Fortune.* (Cassava Republic Press. Abuja, Nigeria. 2013). Page 32

On December 31, 1983, just three months after the return to power of the NPN government, the military took over the government. It was a bloodless coup. Major General Muhammadu Buhari was announced as the new Head of State. His assistant was Brigadier Tunde Idiagbon. The persons that led this coup were Maj. Gen. Ibrahim Babangida, Brigadier Sani Abacha, Brigadier Ibrahim Bako (who was killed during a slight shoot out at the Government House, while seeking to arrest Shagari), Lt. Col. Halilu Akilu, Lt. Col. David Mark, Lt. Col. Tunde Ogbeha, Majo Sambo Dasuki, Major. Abdumummuni Aminu, Major Lawan Gawadabe, and Major Mustapha Haruna Jokolo.

These men felt that Buhari, who claimed not to have known that a coup was in the offing, was popular in the army and was known to be incorruptible and was thus chosen to lead the new government. The people rejoiced over the return to power of the military. But as events would show in the days to come, Nigerians rejoiced too early.

The Babangida Coup

The Buhari administration began on a note of anti-corruption. It immediately detained most politicians of the second republic and set up tribunals, headed by military men, to prosecute these men. While indeed the allegations of corruption was proven against many of them, the tribunal's sentenced many of them to as much as 21-years imprisonment. The Buhari government also set out to arrest Umaru Dikko, the alleged most corrupt politician under Shagari.

Dikko had fled Nigeria to the United Kingdom but the Buhari administration went after him. There was a foiled attempt to kidnap Dikko and return him to Nigeria to answer to charges of corruption. The Israeli mercenaries that sought to kidnap him were discovered at Stansted Airport in Essex. Dikko, who had been drugged, was rescued by British law enforcement. Nigeria was fingered as being behind his ordeal but the Buhari government denied any involvement. This created diplomatic row between Nigeria and Britain.

As long as Buhari fought corruption with Nigeria, the military boys

---

[17] *ThisDay* Newspapers of February 12th, 2009.

who brought him to power had no problem with him. However, Babangida began to have trouble with Buhari when it was discovered that Buhari was setting up mechanism to investigate him on some allegations of corruption. On August, 25, 1985, having been in power for a little less than two years, the Buhari/Idiagbon regime was overthrown. Babangida made this statement in a nationwide address following the coup:

> *"Let me at this point attempt to make you understand the premise upon which it became necessary to change the leadership. The principles of discussions, consultation and co-operation which should have guided the decision-making process of the Supreme Military Council and the Federal Executive Council were disregarded soon after the government settled down in 1984... it turned out that Maj. General Muhammadu Buhari was too rigid and uncompromising in his attitudes to issues of national significance. Efforts to make him understand that a diverse polity like Nigeria required recognition and appreciation of differences in both cultural and individual perceptions, only served to aggravate these attitudes... Maj. Gen. Tunde Idiagbon was similarly inclined in that respect. As Chief of Staff, Supreme Headquarters, he failed to exhibit the appropriate disposition demanded by his position...[18]"*

The story of Babangida's stay in power will be relayed in a later chapter. Suffice to say that all the aforementioned men, who had removed Shagari from power, felt that Buhari was not giving them the leeway they needed in government. Thus they removed him and his deputy from power and sought to rule the nation by themselves.

Other Coups

Mamman Vatsa: On December 23, 1985, a group of soldiers led by

---

[18] Siollun, Max. *Soldiers of Fortune.* (Cassava Republic Press. Abuja, Nigeria. 2013). Page 57

Major Usman Kalabo Bello arrived Maj. Gen. Mamman Vatsa's home in Ikoyi. They had with them a warrant to arrest him. He had been implicated in an investigation into a coup. This was a little more than three months into the Babangida's administration. As of the time of his arrest, Vatsa was the Minister of the Federal Capital City, Abuja. In fact, he was the person who began the full scale development of Abuja under the Babangida administration because his boss had made it clear to him that the country needed to move the nation's capital from Lagos to Abuja as soon as it was practically possible.

Vatsa was the last person anyone could consider would plot a coup against Babangida. Babangida and Vatsa were childhood friends, having attended the same secondary school together in Niger State. They were also course mates in the military. When the rumor of the coup became rife, prior to his arrest, Vatsa had confronted Babangida in the company of two of their friends and asked:

> *"You heard I was planning a coup and couldn't even ask me. What kind of friend are you?" Babangida replied "I didn't believe it. Or are you planning a coup?" Vatsa replied in the negative.*[19]

However, on December 20, 1985, Maj. Gen. Domkat Bali announced to the nation that some officers and men of the military have been discovered to be planning to overthrow the government of Babangida. Vatsa was arrested three days later.

Mamman Vatsa was known as the Poet Soldier. He had written a number of Poems and sent them to the Nigerian Arts and Culture Journal. The editor of that journal was Chinua Achebe. Vatsa would eventually publish a number of books and even won awards for his writings. When the story of his involvement in a coup broke, Professor Wole Soyinka, Chinua Achebe and a number of literary giants in Nigeria, approached the Babangida government and pleaded for his life to be spared.

Babangida promised that he would do all that he can to save him. Vatsa and 13 other officers were put before a military tribunal. After a

---

[19] Siollun, Max. *Soldiers of Fortune.* (Cassava Republic Press. Abuja, Nigeria. 2013). Page 78

lengthy prosecution, Vatsa and the other men were found guilty of wanting to overthrow the Babangida government on the 25th of February, 1986. Vatsa and 9 other officers were executed on the 5th of March, 1986. The other four officers had their sentences commuted to various prison terms.

The case that was brought against Mamman Vatsa was a very weak one. While indeed there may have been a talk of coup among some officers, Vatsa was implicated only because he loaned one of such officers money. Other people think that some middle Belt officers in the Babangida's administration also insisted that Vatsa must die because he was the secretary of the military tribunal that tried Dimka and other Middle Belt officers in 1976. These officers sought revenge for their comrades that were killed in that coup attempt. The death of Mamman Vatsa still remains a stain in the annals of Nigeria's military history.

Gideon Orka: On the night of April 22nd, 1990, soldiers with heavy artillery and weapons converged on Dodan Barracks, the seat of the Nigerian government. General Ibrahim Badamosi Babangida was at home. At the first sounds of gunshots and artillery exchange between these soldiers and the personal guards of Babangida, the Supreme Commander sent his ADC, Usman Kalabo Bello, to find out what was happening. He never saw Bello alive again. Bello was shot dead by the mutinous soldiers.

The main plotters of the April 1990 coup were Major Gideon Orkar, Lt. Col. Anthony Nyiam, Major Saliba Mukoro, Major Cyril Obahor and Captains Harley Empire and Sowaribi Tofolari. The main twist with what has now been now as the Gideon Orkar coup was that all of the perpetrators were from the Niger Delta. Lt. Echendu was the officer in charge of armored personnel at Dodan Barracks and he was the one that led the attack on the home of the President of Nigeria.

When fighting at Dodan Barracks got too fierce, Babangida was persuaded by his security to leave the Barracks. He and his wife, Maryam, with their six month old baby, were driven to a safe house in Surulere Lagos. Attacks were launched at other military barracks around Lagos, including Ikeja Cantonment. The coup plotters, being middle service officers, had the task of dislodging a host of senior officers. This was what made the coup even bloodier.

Unfortunately for the coup plotters, they could not get Maj. Gen. Sanni Abacha. He would eventually prove to be the pivotal figure that made the coup fail. When Abacha eluded the mutineers at his home, he managed to rally troops along with armored carriers. The mutineers could not access as many ammunitions as they wanted and time was running out. Gideon Orkar had gone to the radio to announce the takeover of government. But this was a hasty action because his own men had not succeeded in their various assigned duties. The coup would eventually fail and most of the men involved in it were arrested, tried and executed. Their execution took place on the 27th of July, 1990.

Sanni Abacha: Maj. Gen. Sanni Abacha rose to prominence in the Nigerian military after the Gideon Orkar coup. He was the person who single handedly led the squashing of the coup. Babangida would forever hold him in esteem and gratitude for this. After the April 1990 coup, the Babangida government undertook the mass retirement of a number of army officers. Yet, the Head of State would not retire Abacha. At about the time of the Orka coup, the country's agitation for a return to civilian rule had reached a feverish state. Babangida had conducted a transition program in 1990, only to have the whole process canceled. Politicians were banned and fresh politicking began.

In 1992, the Babangida government approved two political parties: the Social Democratic Party (SDP) and the National Republican Convention (NRC). Chief M.K.O Abiola emerged as the presidential flag bearer for the SDP and Alhaji Tofa was the flag bearer for NRC. The Nigerian nation proceeded to elect a president on June 12, 1993. The election is regarded as the freest and fairest election in the history of Nigeria.

Yet, the Babangida government annulled this election. This singular action would make for the government of Babangida to become extremely unpopular. The clamor for civilian rule would cause Babangida to "step aside" (retire) from government. He formed an interim government to oversee the country and that was to be headed by Chief Ernest Shonekan. In November, 1993, Maj. Gen. Sanni Abacha took over the running of government from Ernest Shonekan. The Abacha coup would be the last successful coup in Nigeria's history.

The Rule of Law

The careful reader may want to ask: is there one single factor that led to the emergence of the military in the annals of Nigeria's history? One may respond to such a question by pointing to the rule of law. Military rule, anywhere in the world, is an illegal rule. It is the ruling of a people by the barrel of the gun and it is an evil thing indeed.

But the military emerged into the Nigerian political scene after Nigeria's politicians themselves began to make nonsense of the laws of the country. The moment the Balewa government began to flout court orders, it left itself vulnerable to be attacked. Victor Banjo, a military officer in the Nigerian army, after his arrest for his alleged involvement in the January 1966 coup, made this point clear in a letter he wrote to Ironsi, from his prison room in Ikot-Epene. Banjo wrote:

> *"No one holds rank and authority in any army by divine right. The relationship of rank and authority in armies are based on law and a definite set of rules and regulations which predetermine the rights and responsibilities at each rank. It is also based on ageless traditions of honor, integrity and loyalty which is expected in reciprocal forms from All Ranks. There is no provision either in an organized state or an organized army for a relaxation of these principles, for on it rests your command, your stability, and your safety; as otherwise there is little to prevent any two officers backed with weapons from arresting any of your officers tomorrow, even your military governors or even yourself...[20]"*

Banjo's words put the matter of authority in any government in perfect perspective. It is the rule of law that upholds society. Where a government disobeys the rule of law, it is opening itself to others who may wish to do so too. The army is only one out of hundreds of other professionals in the country.

The advantage that they have is that the nation has committed its

---

[20] Banjo, Victor; Omigbodun, Olayinka. *A Gift of Sequence.* (Mosuro Publishers. Ibadan, Nigeria. 2008). Page 53

weaponry in their hands to safeguard the people. It is a travesty of duty for the army to then take that same weapon to rule and oppress the people. The military itself knew that its government was illegal and that was why any time they came to power, they gave the impression that they were coming to stabilize the polity; only for them to remain in power for an endless period.

Today, Nigeria has experienced quite a number of civilian to civilian transition of power. We can say that democracy is taking root in our nation today. But each time our government fails to obey court orders or each time they disobey the very laws of the land they have sworn to uphold, they put our democracy at peril.

The only basis for which anyone can talk about ruling another is if they show by example that they are men and women committed to keeping the laws of the land. Coups thrived in Nigeria in the years gone by because our leaders were not committed to the rule of law. Nzeogwu and his friends overthrew the Balewa government because they believed that the government was not committed to keeping the laws of the land.

CHAPTER FOUR

DISCOVERING OIL AND ENDEMIC CORRUPTION

In 1995, the case that the Federal Government of Nigeria brought against Ken Saro-Wiwa and his eight other colleagues, who were members of the Movement for the Survival of Ogoni People (MOSOP), got the attention of the international community. Saro-Wiwa was a businessman, playwright and poet. He however had great concern for the environmental degradation that had hit his homeland, the land of Ogoni, in Rivers State.

He and others therefore launched a non-violent campaign against Shell Petroleum Development Company (SPDC) and the Federal Government of Nigeria, calling on them to ensure that oil exploration in Nigeria was done according to international best practices; so that communities hosting these oil explorers would not continue to suffer degradation. Udeme Epko writes on the consequences of oil exploration on lands in the Niger Delta:

> *"For the oil-bearing communities in the Niger Delta, however, oil has been more of a curse than a blessing. In communities where oil exploration and production are carried out onshore, deforestation, erosion and destroyed farmlands, are the main signposts for this gift of nature. Oil production activities in these communities have*

polluted creeks and destroyed aquatic life. And where there are spillages, losses could be unquantifiable, even where attempts are made by the companies to pay monetary compensation. There is also the problem of acid rain, which destroys houses, which people living within the vicinity of oil exploration and production activities have to contend with every day of their lives.[21]"

This is what MOSOP and the Ogoni people were clamoring against when they came head to head with the government of Nigeria. The Nigerian Head of State in 1995 was General Sanni Abacha. He was a ruthless no-nonsense General in the Nigerian army. Abacha set up a military task force in the Niger Delta that practically stilled every voice of opposition in that part of the country. Yet, men like Saro-Wiwa would not stop speaking.

When government could not still the voice of the Ogoni people, it decided to divide their ranks. It is alleged that some elders in Ogoni land were bribed by both the government of Nigeria and Shell to drop the agitation against Shell explorations of oil on Ogoni land. One day, some of these elders went to the paramount ruler of Ogoni land for a meeting. Some youths learnt of this meeting and invaded the palace. A number of these elders were gruesomely murdered in the pandemonium that followed.

The government of Sanni Abacha held MOSOP responsible for the killing of these men. Saro-Wiwa and ten others were arrested by the Nigerian government and tried by a military tribunal for this crime. Nine of them were found guilty; only one person was acquitted. The whole world called on the Nigerian government to forgive these men and at the least commute the death sentences passed on them to life imprisonment.

Abacha turned a deaf ear on everyone, including the international community, and ordered that all nine Ogoni men, including Saro-Wiwa be executed. Ken Saro-Wiwa and eight other Ogoni elders, known today as Ogoni Nine, were gruesomely hanged on the 10th of November, 1995, by the Sanni Abacha government.

---

[21] Epko, Udeme. The Niger Delta and Oil Politics. (International Energy Communication Limited. Victoria Island, Lagos. 2004). Page 39

Discovery of Oil in Nigeria

When the Europeans came to Nigeria, they were convinced that besides other natural resources they could get off the African soil, they also believed that there was crude oil beneath the land surface of Nigeria. With the coming of the industrial revolution and the making of automobiles, there was an increasing demand for gas (from crude oil) to power these vehicles. For fifty years, the Europeans searched the Nigerian surface but did not find oil.

Such was their relief, however, when on the 30th of April, 1956, crude oil was found in a community called Oloibiri, in the then-Rivers State which is now presently in Bayelsa State. It was discovered by the Shell Petroleum Development Company (SPDC) in commercial quantities. This would begin the long years of oil exploration in the Niger Delta areas of Nigeria. This discovery by Shell spurred other oil companies to embark on massive search for oil deposits in the Niger Delta and with time, more oil discoveries were found not just onshore but also off the shores of the coast of Nigeria.

When the civil war broke out, the main reason why the Biafran Government of Ojukwu was quite confident to face Nigeria was because of the possibility of annexing the Niger Delta's oil wealth under its belt. The government of Yakubu Gowon preempted this move by Ojukwu and therefore divided the Eastern Region into three parts, giving autonomy to Rivers State – the very part of the country where the nation's oil wealth was situated. This, more than any other factor, is what drove Ojukwu to announce his secession from Nigeria on 30th May, 1967. It was however too late because the Nigerian government had already secured the cooperation of the people of the Niger Delta by granting them their own state. At the peak of the war, Nigeria used its access into the Niger Delta to invade Biafra and subsequently defeat Ojukwu.

Oil Wealth

Since 1960, Nigeria is believed to have earned no less than $600 billion in oil revenue. Nigeria is the largest producer of oil in Africa with an estimated volume of 2.413 million barrel per day. Most of the nation's oil reserves are in the Niger Delta area of the country but in recent time, oil companies have found that exploration off the shores of Nigeria were more lucrative for them.

These oil explorations are less subjected to attacks by local vandals but they are more difficult to be monitored by the government of Nigeria. At the same time, such offshore installations were more expensive to install and maintain. When there arose more and more campaigns against oil exploration in the Niger Delta, the oil companies therefore resorted to offshore explorations.

Right now while Nigeria may be earning foreign exchange from oil exporting, no one knows exactly how much oil multinationals are raking off Nigeria. This has necessitated the institution of the Petroleum Industry Bill (PIB) by the Nigerian National Petroleum Corporation (NNPC), the body in charge of managing Nigeria's oil. Unfortunately this bill, which has elements in it that would ensure greater accountability by oil multinationals in Nigerian, has not been able to be passed by the Nigerian Legislative houses because our legislators are either incompetent or bugged down by corruption.

Some have looked on the oil blessing on Nigeria from the point of view of something called a *"resource curse"*. The resource curse theory holds that there is a paradox in countries that seem to have a lot of resources but tend to have less economic growth, less democracy and worse developmental index among its people. Nigeria, since discovering her oil wealth, has also come under this resource curse.

With the advent of oil, there has been less commitment by government and individuals to develop the nation's hitherto thriving agricultural sector. There is a tendency for more and more Nigerians to pursue government jobs, which the Nigerian government could afford to create sometimes in the 1970s because of its enormous wealth. So that a culture of a pursuit of white collar jobs has invaded the minds of young Nigerians and very few people are concerned with attempting the risk in entrepreneurship.

However, with the decline in oil revenue, Nigerians are having to now retrace their steps to agriculture and entrepreneurship. Despite the decline in oil production and revenue earned from oil in the country, Nigeria remains one of the leading oil producers in the world today.

Corruption

With the discovery of oil, also came the unfortunate mismanagement of the resources that accrued from it. One of the leading ways Nigeria mismanaged its resources has been through the endemic corruption embedded in the very fabric of our national life. Corruption may be said to be Nigeria's leading problem. Corruption lies at the root of every malady that has afflicted this giant of the black race, and has transformed her into a giant with clay feet.

When you tell foreigners that you are a Nigerian, the first impression that comes to their mind is SCAM. We have become internationally renowned for corruption and fraudulent activities. Corruption doesn't just apply to the leadership alone but also to the followership. Almost every citizen of Nigeria is engaged in one fraudulent act or another. Those who abstain could probably be because they lack the opportunity to steal.

Chapter 2 Section 15 subsection 5 of the Constitution of the Federal Republic of Nigeria states inter alia: "… the state shall abolish all corrupt practices and abuses of power…" This constitutional stipulation is more often than not observed in the breach by elected politicians and other public office holders in Nigeria. According to a report from the United Nations Office on Drugs and Crime (UNODC) in 2007, over $400 billion dollars was stolen by Nigeria's leaders between 1960 and 1999.

Such a humongous sum of money, if channeled to its rightful purpose, is more than enough to transform Nigeria into El Dorado. This abuse of power is observed in almost all government institutions in Nigeria. General Sani Abacha stole the equivalent of 2% to 3% of Nigeria's GDP for every year that he was Head of State. In the year 2012, a Gallup poll found that 94% of Nigerians thought that corruption was widespread in their government.

The spoils of political corruption -- billions of dollars -- are stashed in foreign bank accounts. The Central Bank of Nigeria in 2013 reported that 76% of the country's crude oil revenue, intended for the bank, was unaccounted for. Nigeria's current President, Muhammadu Buhari, is doing his best to stymie the high rate of corruption in Nigeria.

A lot of money that was stolen in times past by politicians and other public office holders, which were stashed in foreign banks, have been returned to the country and not a few who perpetuated such heist are either undergoing prosecution by the anti-graft agencies or have been convicted by the courts and are currently serving jail time.

Electoral corruption is a subset of corruption which we must not gloss over as this makes it possible for the bad guys to get to power. Vote rigging, vote buying, ballot box snatching, threats, intimidation and electoral violence are just a few of the ills that currently plague our electoral processes and serve as a catalyst to political corruption. We must sanitize our electoral process if we are truly desirous of minimizing corruption in our society.

There is also corruption among the followership. No matter your qualifications, it is almost an impossibility to get a job in Nigeria if you don't have a godfather. Getting a job which can pay the bills and enable you to afford some luxuries is now a matter of "man-know-man" as it is said in local parlance.

Gender discrimination is also rife in the country. Most women cannot get good jobs or contracts without the exchange of sexual favours. This includes securing promotion in the workplace if they are eventually employed. There is also the issue of disparity in wages between male and female employees though it is a global phenomenon that isn't peculiar to Nigeria.

The Press, which is the fourth estate of the realm, has a constitutionally enshrined role to hold the leaders accountable to the people by acting as the watchdog of the society. Poor pay, delayed payment of salaries, allowances (for several months and sometimes years), and rising costs of living has made many journalists to abdicate this all-important role.

Many journalists in Nigeria are currently on the payroll of politicians whom they are supposed to hold accountable when they are perceived to have engaged in acts of corruption and abuse of power. This unfortunate practice has led to the production of weak and biased news reports, the glorification of political villains, and the dearth of investigative journalism in Nigeria. Not a few political pundits, commentators and watchers have opined that the corruption in the private sector is worse than that which exists in the public sector.

It is the sad and absolute reality prevalent in our clime. Many businessmen and professionals collude with politicians to fleece the country. Nigerian banks are a cesspool of corruption as they are the principal instruments through which stolen money is laundered overseas. Bankers are often the ones who teach the politicians all the tricks in the books to stash stolen money overseas without it being flagged or tracked.

They know all the measures to take that would not violate any global banking and international finance laws. Many businessmen serve as fronts for corrupt politicians, helping them to hide their loot through the creation of fake companies, anonymous ownership of shares in their companies, and storing of looted funds in their personal bank accounts. Some corrupt businessmen also specialize in the importation and production of fake products, the use of cheap labour, and the production of inferior goods which is often passed off as superior goods with the aim of defrauding the consumer.

Another set of people who aid corrupt politicians are the civil servants. At the inception of the Buhari administration in 2015, many civil servants were hauled before anti-corruption agencies for investigation and prosecution after large sums of money were found in their bank accounts and personal houses. These civil servants could not justify or explain their wealth in relation to their salaries and allowances.

Civil servants enjoy anonymity and permanence of tenure which enables them to be in office for several years, looting and enabling the politicians to loot the exchequer without qualms. The media and the general public focus all their attention on the politicians and other public office holders, overlooking the civil servant without whom no politician or public servant can steal a dime from the public till.

Effects of Corruption on the Citizenry

Ignorance of the effects of corruption on the citizenry is the reason why many Nigerians not only condone corruption by the elite, but also defend their actions and celebrate them as heroes. Some cannot connect the dots and see the nexus between corruption in high places and the poverty in their personal lives. My aim is to enlighten Nigerians on the deleterious effects of corruption on their personal lives, and in the process prove that all we need to do to make Nigeria great again is to minimize corruption in our society. A country like Nigeria with a very high degree of corruption will have very few people investing in it, and this includes both local and foreign investors. This is because every investor desires profit and not loss.

Even those who engage in corruption know this to be true. That is why more often than not, they are quick to stash their stolen funds and assets overseas to the detriment of their home countries. Capital flight and lack of investments will lead to loss of jobs and a general increase in the labour market. When funds which should have been invested in the productive sectors of the economy are looted by public office holders, the result is a general rise in poverty among the citizenry.

For example, different governments at various times in Nigeria have come up with economic empowerment schemes to empower indigent citizens and promote entrepreneurship among the populace, especially among the youths. These funds would eventually be misappropriated and mismanaged, and the end users (citizens) never get anything substantial out of it. A recent example is the SURE-P Program of the Goodluck Jonathan administration.

Corruption hampers national development. It discourages industry and honesty which affects national productivity and development. Bribery adds to the cost of production which inevitably leads to an increase in the prices of goods and services, and reduces the purchasing power of the consumers. This is harmful to the economy. Also, corruption leads to leakages in the economy and does not make for effective economic planning, which subsequently affects the quality of life of the people.

Corruption introduces distortion in the society. It makes some to become excessively rich while the majority becomes excessively poor. This disrupts consumption patterns which is not in the national economic interest. That is the reason we have a high rate of crime, terrorism, banditry etc. An army of extremely poor people is fodder for criminal and terrorist organizations, who lure them into their folds with the promise of quick riches and other material gains. Corruption creates distortion in the polity as only the affluent show some degree of patriotism because of what they stand to lose should the country fail and totally disintegrate.

A summation of the message that I am trying to pass across is this: that the first and greatest effect of corruption on the citizens of any society is POVERTY. When the resources that belong to the majority are cornered by the minority, the majority suffers.

Ending Graft in Nigeria

The government of Chief Olusegun Obasanjo, at its inception in 1999, recognized the debilitating effects of corruption on Nigeria. To strengthen its campaign against graft in the country, Obasanjo decided to upgrade the anti-graft unit of the Nigerian police from a mere department under the police and made it into an agency.

Thus began the Economic and Financial Crimes Commission (EFCC), led then by its pioneer chairman, Malam Nuhu Ribadu. The EFCC under Ribadu and his successors, was and is still quite effective in nabbing corrupt public officials in Nigeria. A couple of former governors are currently cooling their heels in prison after their were convicted by the courts for corruption.

Victory in the anti-graft war would not mean the total elimination of corruption in the Nigerian society. Indeed there is no country that is totally free from corruption. What is desired is the minimization or a huge reduction of corruption or corruption-related activities in Nigeria. Corruption must cease to be a way of life for our people. It must be seen as an aberrant behaviour with shameful and punitive consequences when the perpetrator is caught regardless of his/her status in the society.

I must also not fail to point out that the focus of both the previous and current administration's war on graft has been one-sided. The focus has always been on the leaders and not the led. That is the wrong approach. Every political leader today was once a follower yesterday. The leadership of any nation is often a reflection of the dominant character of its people. No leader in Nigeria can rise above the general and collective aspirations, proclivities and tendencies of the majority.

It is a sad and unfortunate reality that the average Nigerian breathes, eats, sleeps, and dreams corruption in his daily life, yet he expects the leaders of the nation to act differently from him when they have the keys to the government coffers.

The number one thing that all Nigerians need to know is that winning the anti-graft war is a collaborative effort between the leaders and the led. While the leaders show leadership, the followers are expected to show followership by emulating them. Since the advent of the Fourth Republic, the Obasanjo administration and the Buhari administration have made attempts to fight corruption.

Did they get any support from the citizenry? The answer is capital NO. Rather the view held by a majority of Nigerians is that the fight against corruption is a witch hunt targeted at the political enemies of both Presidents. Even when the majority of those arrested by the anti-graft agencies during the Obasanjo administration were members of his own party, the Peoples' Democratic Party (PDP).

Many will also support the government clampdown on corrupt politicians until a member of their family, kinsman, tribe, or region, is enmeshed in a corruption scandal. Then they will turn around and join the majority to chorus that it is a witch hunt.

Every Nigerian should eschew corruption in their daily lives. Let's stop cheating and defrauding our fellow citizens when we engage in business and other economic activities. Gone are those days when people used to place goods in front of their houses or shops unmonitored, and go to their farms. And the buyer will come and pick whatever he/she desires, put the money on the table and walked away. The seller would return from the farm and find his/her money safe and intact.

Those were the good old days when honesty, integrity, and accountability was the watchword of almost all citizens of the country. Today, people are ready to engage in all manner of criminal and fraudulent activities against their fellow citizens in order to get ahead in life. Yet, they are quick to blame the government when things are not working as they should in the country.

The whistleblower policy of the Buhari administration, though novel to our clime, is nonetheless an ingenious attempt at making Nigerians more socially responsible in the fight against graft. The anti-graft and security agencies are not spirits who are expected to know everything going on in the country. It is human beings like you and I that give them information which they act upon.

For example, if you know someone who was living in a 3-bedroom rented apartment before he entered public service, and suddenly builds a $1 million dollars house in just three months in office, the right and proper thing to do is to inform the anti-graft agencies to probe the source of his sudden wealth. While some might lampoon such citizens as poke nosing in the affairs of others, he/she would not only have satisfied their conscience but would have also made an invaluable contribution to the development and betterment of the society.

That is how citizens of technologically and economically advanced nations operate and we wonder why their society seems almost perfect. Our Judiciary needs to be sanitized and strengthened so as to ensure a smooth and successful prosecution of those indicted for corruption. Else, what will happen is what we are currently experiencing where the EFCC and ICPC would arrest alleged looters of public funds, and the Judiciary would set such individuals free based on either a technicality or insufficient evidence as they often claim.

The anti-graft agencies need to be properly funded to make their staff immune to bribes from those under investigation and so that they can be equipped with modern technological gadgets which aid in the investigation and prosecution of corruption cases. Similarly, heads of anti-graft agencies should be appointed strictly on merit. Staff of these agencies should enjoy permanence of tenure like civil servants.

The media and government agencies like the National Orientation Agency (NOA) should embark on a massive sensitization campaign with specific emphasis on the rural areas where poverty and ignorance is rife. This will enlighten the citizenry about the harmful effects of corruption not just in the society alone but also in their personal lives.

The messages must be vivid, direct, clear, and concise in order to make those at the bottom of the ladder in the society see how corruption is responsible for their failures in life. This will curb the tendency to hero-worship corrupt politicians who give them handouts and stipends occasionally, in order to buy their conscience and support during elections.

Religion is a vital and important aspect in the life of an average Nigerian. Karl Marx was right when he opined that *"Religion is the opium of the masses"*. Politicians use religion as a tool to further keep the masses in captivity by aligning themselves with the religious leaders who wields great power over the congregants. They give these religious leaders large sums of money to fund projects. They give them gifts like cars, houses, private jets, etc., so as to buy their conscience and secure their endorsements during the period of electioneering.

There needs to be a paradigm shift on the part of the religious leaders if we truly desire to win the anti-graft war. Our Pastors, Imams, and Traditionalists should endeavour to preach the truth at all times. They should speak truth to power and harp more on values like love, honesty, integrity, thrift, fairness etc. Religious leaders should not be dwelling excessively on prosperity and materialism in their sermons to the laity.

There needs to be proper government funding of schools, most especially the tertiary institutions. An overhaul of the educational curriculum with a strong emphasis on skills acquisition and development is an absolute necessity. This will develop self-reliance and entrepreneurship in our youths and keep them engaged in positive and productive ventures. An idle mind is the devil's workshop remains a relevant truism in our country. An engaged mind is less likely to engage in fraud or corruption. Finally, the government must ensure that there is equality before the law when it comes to the anti-graft war. There should be no sacred cows and anyone found guilty by a court of law should be made to face the music to serve as a deterrent to others.

CHAPTER FIVE

IBB

In January, 1976, Ibrahim Badamasi Babandiga (IBB) was promoted to the rank of a full colonel by the administration of Muritala Muhammad. Babangida had been one of the northern officers that had worked with Muritala to oust General Yakubu Gowon in a bloodless coup on July 29, 1975. The Muritala government therefore rewarded Babangida with not only a promotion but also included him in the Supreme Military Council (SMC), the highest decision making body in the country. Babangida was only 34-years old.

On the morning of 13th February, 1976, Col. Babangida had woken up early at his 19, Ikoyi Crescent, home on the island of Lagos. The previous day, he had instructed his driver and army assistants to arrive early at his home because of a crucial meeting that was billed to hold that Friday morning at the Supreme Headquarters of the army in Dodan Barracks.

At about half past eight that morning, Babangida and his military entourage set out for work in one vehicle. Babangida talks about that fateful morning:

> *I was living at No. 19 Ikoyi Crescent and in setting out to Defence Headquarters, my driver could either take the right and go on to Osborne road or take a left and go on to Kingsway Road. On this morning, as I saw him indicating a right turn, by sheer happenstance... I don't*

> *know when I said, no, go left. And that was how we just avoided the path of danger[22].*

A few minutes after Babangida had arrived at the office, he received a phone call from his immediate boss, the Chief of Army Staff, Lt. Gen. Theophilus Danjuma. Danjuma informed Babangida that there has been a mutiny in the army and that the Head of State, Gen. Muritala Muhammed had been shot, with the likelihood that he had been killed. He immediately instructed Babangida to gather troops and go and dislodge the mutinous soldiers who were at the National Broadcasting Corporation (NBC).

Babangida would later learn that his close friend, Lt. Col. Buka Suka Dimka, was the ringleader of the group at the NBC. Babangida's first instinct was to go and bombard the NBC and smoke the mutinous soldiers out. Later, as he was being driven through the deserted streets of Lagos, he thought that he could confront Dimka and talk him into surrendering. This way, they could avoid further bloodletting.

Babangida arrived the NBC fully kitted but he requested his driver to stop one street to his destination. He removed his gun and left it in the car and then proceeded to the broadcasting station. As he approached the NBC building, a young soldier accosted him and demanded where he was going. This soldier knew he was talking to Col. Babangida but in times of coup, the person with the gun is the one with greater authority.

Babangida had his hands up and requested to see the soldier's commanding officer. At about the time Babangida was conversing with this soldier, Dimka spotted them from inside the building. Immediately he motioned to the soldier, a sentry, to allow Babangida come in. When Babangida stepped into the building, he noticed that the whole place was in disarray. Many of the soldiers, including Dimka, were drunk and any slight altercation could provoke shooting. Babangida realized that his task was cut out for him.

Immediately he said to Dimka: *"your coup has been aborted..."*

"What do you mean aborted?" Dimka retorted. *"Muritala is dead."*

---

[22] Umoden, Gabriel. E. *The Babangida Years...* Page 29

"Yes," Babangida responded, *"but all the other generals are still alive."*

"We would get them also…"

"Dimka, face the reality on ground: in a matter of minutes, this place would be surrounded with troops and your men would either be killed or arrested."

"Don't threaten me Ibrahim."

"It is not a threat. It is the reality. Why don't you guys give up your arms and then let us work out a middle position with the army authorities. General Danjuma is willing to talk to you."

"Fuck Danjuma and his whole lineage…" Dimka said with disgust.

Then he realized that there could be some wisdom in the words of Babangida.

"Tell Danjuma to write a letter on his official letterhead that my boys and I would be granted amnesty if we surrender."

Babangida thought about it for a minute and said he would get back to Dimka. With that short discussion, he stormed out of the NBC building. When Babangida reported to Theophilus Danjuma, the Chief of Army Staff would have none of such negotiations. He reminded Babangida that he had instructed him to dislodge Dimka from the NBC and not to go have a tete-a-tete with him.

Babangida returned to the NBC, this time with troops and a gun battle broke out. In a little over two hours, Dimka's men were subdued. But despite the fact that the NBC building was surrounded by troops, Lt. Col. Dimka got away from the whole melee. Babangida would later discover that he was one of the prime targets of the coup plotters but his last minute decision to take another route to the office helped evade his killers.

Most of those who carried out the coup that led to the assassination of Gen. Muritala Muhammed were friends of Babangida. He never could understand why his own friends would want him dead. The January 1976 coup created an impression in Babangida's mind that even his closest friends in the army could not be trusted.The dislodging of the coup plotters from the NBC building by this fair skinned, gapped teeth, military officer launched Babangida into national consciousness. He became a subject of discussion by the Nigerian Press.

Babangida's Early Life

Ibrahim Badamasi Babangida was born on August 17th, 1941. His parents were Gwari from present day Niger State. Babangida was the eldest of six children but only one of his siblings, Hannatu Bello, survived infancy. Babangida's childhood was one founded in much sorrow as his father died when Babangida was only six years old. Shortly after his mother died also. Babangida and his younger sister were sent to live with relatives, which incidentally turned out to be the household of Abdulsalam Abubakar – another future Head of State in Nigeria.

Babangida began his primary school education at the Native Authority School in Minna in 1950. His classmate was Abdusalam Abubakar. In 1956, Babangida and Abdulsalami gained admission to Government College, Bida. While at school, army recruiters would usually come to the school to encourage the students to make a career in the nation's army. In 1957, during one of such visits by the recruiters, a young, slim and smartly dressed Nigerian army officer also came along with the recruiters to Babangida's school.

The students were promised that if they make a career in the Nigerian army, they could become like this army officer. The students were greatly moved by the sight of this officer and it is likely many of them, at that point, made up their minds to join the army. The young officer that came with the recruiters that day was Lieutenant Yakubu Gowon. Babangida and fifteen other classmates of his sat for the exams to join the Nigerian Military Training College (NMTC) in Kaduna in 1962.

Eleven of them passed. Some of them will include Abdulsalam Abubakar, Mamman Vatsa, Garba Duba, Gado Nasko, Sani Bello, Mohammed Magoro and Sani Sanni. All of these persons would feature prominently in Nigeria military history in the future. While at NMTC, Babangida met a quiet, young and diminutive Kanuri man from Kano State. His name was Sani Abacha. Babangida and Abacha would form a life-long friendship from that time on.

After his graduation from the NMTC, Babangida went to the Indian Military Academy. His friend, Vatsa, was also on that training. They both graduated in April 1964, after which Babangida was posted to the 1st Reconnaissance Squadron where he served under Major Hassan Katsina. While serving under Katsina, Babangida was a member of the Nigerian army unit sent to the Tiv region to quell rising protests in that part of the country. Babangida was in Kaduna when a section of the military struck on 15th January, 1966. Babangida knew Major Chukwuma Kaduna Nzeogwu very well. In a subsequent interview, Babangida had this to say about the coup:

> *"(The January 15th 1966 coup) was not an Igbo-based thing as far as I could imagine, but the execution of the coup was poorly done and made people think that it was one-sided. I could recall Nzeogwu saying that some chaps in the south let him down because they had not been able to carry out instruction the way he wanted them.[23]"*

This testimony by Babangida lends credence to the position that in the days following the January 15th coup, very few people held the position that the coup was an Igbo coup. Unfortunately the Igbos did not manage their stay in power well under Aguiyi-Ironsi and in no time, the impression that it was an Igbo coup, with the active connivance of Ironsi, had pervaded most of the army, leading to the July 29, 1966 coup. Babangida joined some other young Northern elements in the Nigerian army to carry out the July 29th coup.

During the Nigerian civil war, Babangida commanded the 44th Infantry Battalion. They were nicknamed "The Rangers". Babangida was promoted to the rank of a Captain in August, 1968. Babangida's battalion served under Colnel Muhammad Shuwa's 1st Division. During the war, Babangida was wounded at Uzuakoli in April 1969 and had to be evacuated from the war front. After his wound had healed, Babangida returned to the war front.

The bullet wound to his leg never actually got fixed; Babangida still

---

[23] Newswatch magazine. January 8, 1990.

endured bouts of pain in that leg even when he was Head of State. In 1970, following the war, Babangida was promoted to the rank of Major. He then proceeded to Warminster, UK, for a course and when he returned he was appointed an instructor at the Nigerian Defence Academy (NDA). At the NDA, Babangida was involved in training young military men to join the Nigerian Army.

He however went a little further in this training: Babangida won the life-long support and loyalty of many of these men at this time. These boys would eventually form the caucus that would be known as IBB's boys in the future. One of such men that Babangida taught in 1970 was Abubakar Umar – a future military Governor of Kaduna State. After his stint at the NDA, Babangida was sent for further training in the United States of America. When he returned, he was promoted to the rank of Lt. Colonel in 1974.

On July 29, 1975, Babangida joined Muritala Mohammed to overthrow General Yakubu Gowon in a bloodless coup. Other perpetrators in that coup would include Shehu Musa Yar'Adua, Joseph Garba, Abdullahi Mohammed and Anthony Ochefu. For his role in the army, Babangida was appointed as a member of the Supreme Military Council (SMC). He was also the Inspector of Reece. Babangida was serving in this capacity when the Dimka coup of 1975 occurred.

Babangida's Early Years in Government

Major General Ibrahim Babangida was the Chief of Army Staff under the Gen. Muhammadu Buhari government. But Babangida became disenchanted with the way and manner Buhari was running the country. He held the position that Buhari was too straight-jacketed and that he was arrogating too much powers to Idiagbon who, although was Buhari's deputy, was junior to Babangida and many others in the army.

Babangida and a few others had been the brain behind the December 1983 coup that brought an end to the Shehu Shagari government and they had invited Buhari to come and lead the government. But in the process of ridding the nation of corruption, Buhari was beginning to step on toes in the military. Babangida made indirect statements to

Buhari indicating that he and his boys were not happy. It was even said that Buhari retorted "if they want, they can come and collect their government". And this is exactly what Babangida did. On August 27, 1985,

Babangida led a bloodless coup that toppled Buhari. Buhari was arrested at his home by Majors Abubakar Umar, Lawan Gwadabe, Abdulmumuni Aminu and Sambo Dasuki. Idiagbon had been away to Mecca for Hajj. When he heard of the toppling of his government, he rushed back to Nigeria and was arrested at the airport. Buhari and Idiagbon were detained for two years after this.

As it was with a change of an unpopular government, which the Buhari administration had become in late 1985, Nigerians rejoiced at the toppling of the strict Buhari/Idiagbon regime. Babangida rode under this popularity in the first few years of his government. Political detainees, who had been imprisoned by the Buhari government for corruption or for violating government's policies on the press, were mostly released.

The Nigerian people cheered. Then Babangida proceeded to change many of the nomenclatures in the governing arm of the military government. The SMC was changed to the Armed Forces Ruling Council (AFRC), the Federal Executive Council was renamed the National Council of Ministers, and Supreme Headquarters was given the name General Staff Headquarters.

It appeared that Babangida was carrying out this renaming exercise to remove the hard core military posture that the Nigerian government carried around. Later in his government, Babangida himself would come to be referred as "President" and not "Head of State" as all military leaders before him had been called. And as usual Babangida rewarded all those who helped in installing him to power with juicy positions in government.

In his early days in government, Babangida repealed Decree 4, a policy of repression against press freedom instituted by the Buhari government. He released popular journalists like Tunde Thompson and Nduka Irabor who had been jailed under this decree. In contrast to the stern government of Buhari, Babangida created an informal relationship with the press and this open door policy that they had with him led the press to shower his government with lots of praises in the early days. Babangida suspended the execution of drug peddlers.

He appointed as his deputy an Igbo man – Commodore Ebitu Ukiwe – who was of the Nigerian Navy. With that action, he won the support of the South-East who had been largely ignored in political appointments by subsequent governments since the end of the civil war in 1970. With this action, he won the support of Nigerians from the South-East.

Babangida went on to appoint technocrats into his government: Professors Wole Soyinka, Kalu Idika Kalu, Tam David-West, Bolaji Akinyemi, and Olikoye Ransome-Kuti all worked for him. Some of these individuals served as ministers under the Babangida government. The popularity of the Babangida government at this time is best captured by the word of Larry Diamond, a foreign journalist:

> *"With his intelligence, charisma, and personal charm; his recruitment of outstanding intellectual and technocratic talent; his visionary twin program of transition and structural adjustment; the considerable international sympathy these programs garnered; and the national readiness for serious change after the debacle of the second republic; Ibrahim Babangida, more than any other Nigerian leader, had the potential to lead Nigeria onto a truly different, more civic, and institutional historical path.[24]"*

The first place where Babangida began to lose popularity was the press. Prior to the end of the Buhari government, Babangida had developed a cordial relationship with Dele Giwa who, at that time, was an editor in Moshood Abiola's Sunday Concord. Some have said that Babangida was the one who gave Dele Giwa, Ray Epku, Dan Egbese and Yakubu Mohammed the seed money to start Newswatch. Whatever the story is, Newswatch began to operate in January 1985.

When Babangida came to power in August of that year, Newswatch gave his government lots of positive reviews. But after Newswatch published a story on the Babangida's government introduction of a

---

[24] Diamond, Larry. Transition Without End... **Page 477**

second-tier foreign exchange market, the State Security Services (SSS) called Dele Giwa in for questioning. Things were becoming tense between former friends following this incident.

On Friday, October 17, 1986, Giwa was again invited by the SSS for questioning. Lt. Colonel Togun questioned Giwa on planning to import arms into Nigeria, colluding with student unions to cause a socialist revolution in Nigeria, preparing to feature an article to embarrass government on the exit of CGS Ebitu Ukiwe from the Babangida government, and some other allegations. Giwa denied all of them and at some point he got into a shouting match with Colonel Togun.

On Saturday, October 18, 1986, Dele Giwa's wife, Funmi, received a call from Colonel Halilu Akilu, asking after her husband. He would go on to ascertain the house address of the Giwa from her in that conversation. On Sunday, October 19, 1986, at about 11 am, two men in a white Peugeot 504 arrived Giwa's house. After confirming that Dele Giwa was home, they gave his security guard a parcel that was well banded.

The guard gave the parcel to Giwa's 19-year old son, Billy. Billy took the parcel to his father, who was in his study at the time, and left. Kayode Soyinka, Newswatch London Bureau Chief, was with Giwa in the office. When Dele Giwa received the parcel, he said "this must be from the president". As he made to open the parcel, an explosion ripped through the room. Fire from the explosion badly burned Dele Giwa from his waist downward. Soyinka, who had been sitting opposite Giwa, was thrown out of his seat by the power of the letter bomb.

His hearing was impaired for five years. Sympathizers rushed into Giwa's study and put out the fire, while he was rushed to the hospital where he would later succumb to his wounds. The death of Dele Giwa in October 1986 began to make the Babangida administration unpopular. Later investigations would reveal that Dele Giwa may have been killed because he was working on a sensational story around one Gloria Okon. The Babangida administration vigorously denied any involvement in the death of Dele Giwa.

The Culture of Corruption under Babangida

Ibrahim Babangida's eight year rule brought profound social, economic and political changes to Nigeria. This is why it is impossible to tell the story of modern Nigeria without discussing IBB as one entity in the whole story. Babangida's overriding philosophy to governance was that he needed to do everything to keep himself in power.

Babangida had been involved in every coup in Nigeria, except the Dimka coup, so he understood the psychology of soldiers and what he needed to do to satisfy them so that he could remain in power. In the process, the Babangida administration committed a lot of the nation's resources to the military; largely helping his friends and cronies there to contracts and illegal sums of wealth.

It was in the days of Babangida that "bigmanism" became a full fledge culture in Nigeria. Prior to his administration, military governors and heads of states were simply addressed by their titles. But in Babangida's time, the suffix "Your Excellency" had to be added to these names when they are addressed in public. Babangida's wife, Maryam, took the office of the "First Lady" to a height that had never been witnessed before in the country.

The result was that a culture of corruption and impunity began to thrive in the country. People began to attain heights of wealth without working for it. All one needed to do was to know a "big man" somewhere and doors will simply open. The tendency to earn money without working became a culture in the country; a culture we are yet to be rid of – having metamorphosed to *"yahoo-yahoo"* boys in our own day and time.

In 1990/91, the United States of America led a war against Iraq to defend Saudi Arabia against the incursion of Saddam Hussein into that country. That war is known as the Gulf War. During the crisis, the nations of the world stopped purchasing oil from Iraq and had to rely on other oil producing nations, like Nigeria, to supply them with crude oil. In the process, Nigeria made a lot more than it would normally make; because there was a greater demand, the price of crude oil shot up.

It is believed that the administration of Ibrahim Babangida largely frittered these monies away through corruption. Dr. Pius Okigbo, a renowned economist, headed an investigative panel (instituted by the Sani Abacha regime in 1994) that looked into the extra that Nigeria made in this period. They came out with what is today known as the "Okigbo Report" indicting the Babangida government. A part of the report read thus:

> *"...neither the president (Babangida) nor the (CBN) governor accounted to anyone for these massive extra budgetary expenditures... these disbursements were clandestinely undertaken while the country was reeling with a crushing external debt overhang... These represent... a gross abuse of public trust.[25]"*

It is estimated that a total sum of $12.2 billion was mismanaged by the Babangida administration in this period. The large scale corruption in the Babangida administration would eventually flow from the head to the people. There was very little corruption expose in the media because even the mass media realized that if she would thrive in those days, she would have to turn a deaf ear to corruption.

There was no internet in those days, so the formal print and electronic media (TV and radio) was all that people could rely on to get information. Many of the media institutions in the country became polarized by corrupt elements and tendencies. Even after Babangida's administration, Sani Abacha simply permitted the corrupt culture in society to continue to thrive. It was not until Olusegun Obasanjo and the coming of the EFCC that the country begin to take proactive measures against corruption. By this time the damage had been done. A whole generation of Nigerians had been raised in a culture that was largely characterized by corrupt tendencies. We could say that there was corruption before Ibrahim Babangida but his administration made corruption seem like the norm in Nigeria.

June 12

---

[25] Siollun, Max. *Soldiers of Fortune.* (Cassava Republic Press Book. Abuja, Nigeria. 2013.) page 180

Military governments in Nigeria's history has always regarded itself as an aberration but they remained in power because they gave the impression that they came to sanitize the political system with a plan to return power to civilians as soon as these objectives had be fulfilled. Babangida's government also dangled this carrot of a promised return to civil rule before Nigerians in all of its eight years; it was the only way it could justify its stay in power.

But extended military rule inflicted a damage on the psyche of military men. It created a dichotomy in the Nigerian military where some soldiers were regarded as political and others were simply professional. Political soldiers were those who partook in coups and enjoyed the perks of political offices. These soldiers could be of lower ranks; the fact remained that as long as they had risked their lives to install their boss in power, they were expected to be given political offices.

These men were the ones that became state governors or ministers in the military governments they created. On the other hand the professional soldiers were usually apolitical. They were disciplined men that insisted that politics was destroying professionalism in the Nigerian military. They were also a group that insisted on power being returned to the civilians as soon as it was possible. General Abdulsalami, Babangida's school mate, was one of such apolitical soldiers and Nigeria owes its swift return to civilian rule 1998/99 to this man's professionalism.

To give a semblance of commitment to return to democratic rule, at the inception of his government, Gen. Ibrahim Babangida had created a Political Bureau. It consisted of political science professors and journalists who essentially drew out a program for the nation's return to civilian rule. To be able to achieve their objectives, this group led by Dr. Sylvanus Cookey, went to all the 301 local governments that Nigeria had then, and obtained the opinion of the Nigerian people through fact finding, debates and submission of memoranda.

This bureau submitted its finding to the Babangida government in April 1987 and suggested, among other things, that a two party system should be created for a transition to civilian rule. They also suggested that 1990 will be a fitting date for the military to completely withdraw from politics. Babangida proceeded to allow Nigerians to form political parties but made it clear that the final two would be chosen by the military itself.

After extensive politicking, the military would again reject all the political parties that emerged from these political processes. On May 3, 1989, Babangida announced that the Federal Military Government has agreed to form two parties: the Social Democratic Party (SDP) and the National Republican Party (NRC). This decision opened the gate to full scale politicking as civilians again realigned themselves to different political camps across the nation with the hope of wrestling power completely from the military.

By this time, the Babangida government had gradually began to reduce the number of military men in its administration. In fact at some point in his government, most of Babangida's ministers and state governors were civilians. Yet ultimate powers and authority rested in the hands of the political military men.

On August 1st 1990, the two political parties conducted primary elections to determine who would emerge as their presidential candidates. Alhaji Adamu Ciroma won the ticket for the NRC, while retired Maj. Gen. Shehu Yar'Adua won the ticket for the SDP. But these elections were clearly marred by malpractices and rigging. The Babangida administration saw this and decided to cancel the processes that led to the emergence of these politicians. Some twenty-five leading politicians, including Ciroma and Yar'Adua, that emerged during these political processes were banned. Fresh primaries were again rescheduled for March 1993.

At this point, doubts were emerging from the minds of Nigerians on whether or not Babangida was committed to returning power to the civilians. In fact his frequent banning of politicians and rescheduling of the transition processes earned him the nick-name "Maradona" – after the 1986 Argentine footballer, whose proficiency with the football and ability to score goals, including a very controversial one with the "hand of God", earned him worldwide renown. Babangida was Nigeria's political Maradona of that time.

The March 1993 presidential primaries at the SDP produced Chief Moshood Abiola, a business tycoon, as its presidential candidate. Alhaji Ibrahim Tofa became the presidential candidate for the NRC. Nigerian then proceeded to the polls on June 12, 1993 to elect who would be their President. While elections had always been contentious matters in Nigeria's history up till this time, the June 12 elections were completely different. Nigerians, probably tired of years of military rule and their inability to produce civilian rulers, came out en-masse and voted who would become their President.

For the first time in Nigerian history, the June 12 elections were said to be free, fair and credible. By the close of voting that day, it was obvious to many that Chief Moshood Abiola would emerge the winner of the elections. However, as the politicians rejoiced and Nigerians looked forward to a handing over of power to civilian rule, other intrigues were being played out.

On June 10, 1993, a group called the Association for Better Nigeria (ABN) led by an Igbo business tycoon, Chief Authur Nzeribe, took the National Electoral Committee (NEC) to court, calling for the cancellation of the elections. Justice Ikpeme of an Abuja court granted the ABN their wishes and instructed NEC not to carry on with the elections. Some political military men asked Babangida to bring an end to the electoral processes based on this court ruling but he refused, insisting that the elections must go on.

After the elections, Babangida was again brought under pressure by these political military men, led by Gen. Sanni Abacha, that the transition process should be cancelled. Babangida understood that it was his name and legacy that was being placed on the line if he canceled the elections so he could not do it. It is said that Abacha was particularly against the emergence of Abiola as President. Finally on June 23, 1993, an unsigned press release from the office of the press secretary of the country's Vice-President, Admiral Augustus Aikhomu, said that the June 12, 1993 elections were canceled.

Even Babangida could not come into the public to make this declaration. The Nigerian nation was plunged into crisis with this announcement, with riots occurring in mostly the Southern parts of the country were Abiola was from. However, the decision of the military not to hand-over power to Abiola remained even after Babangida had left power.

Babangida's Latter Days and Legacy

After the June 12 elections were annulled, Babangida urged the SDP and the NRC to submit two members each to him to form an interim government that will oversee another election while he resigns from heading the government. The SDP rejected this proposal firmly. Their position was for the full results of the elections to be announced and for the perceived winner, Abiola, installed as the President of the country.

About this time the ban on politicians was lifted and people like Shehu Yar'Adua were able to make input into the ongoing discussions at federal level. What was clear at about this time was this: while Babangida was willing to hand over power to Abiola, there were element in the military that were strongly against it. One of such was Gen. Sani Abacha. There were also a group of military men who had been too exposed to the perks of political office that were very unwilling to return power to civilians. So while Babangida's transition processes dragged on, these people were doing everything to ensure that there would be no such thing as a return to civilian rule.

By August 1993, the overwhelming agreement among the military and even some politicians, like Yar'Adua and Obasanjo, was for Babangida to leave power. They also agreed that an interim government was to be set up. Obasanjo was approached to head this government but he declined. Then, for some reason, it was agreed that all senior military officers were to resign but that Gen. Sani Abacha was to be the only military officer to remain in the interim government. Chief Ernest Shonekan was appointed to head the interim government. This government's main goal was to oversee another elections in the country.

On August 26, 1993, Gen. Ibrahim Badamosi Babangida "stepped aside". He claimed that military men do not "stepped down" but actually step aside. He had ruled Nigeria for eight years and under him the country had undergone tremendous transformation. To his credit, not everything that Babangida did was evil. Under his administration, the nation's capital city was taken from the loud and over populated Lagos to Abuja – which is termed a "Federal Capital City" (FCT).

Situating the seat of the nation's power on a mountain, surrounded by a rich vegetation, with heavy security, has discouraged coups from taking place. There has been no coup in Nigeria (in the bloody manner) since our capital city was taken to Abuja. It was Babangida that also built the third Mainland Bridge that connects Mainland Lagos to the Island. That bridge stands as a means of decongesting traffic in Lagos and has helped Nigeria's largest capital city thrive economic wise. Lastly, Babangida helped stabilize Nigeria in some very real sense.

Babangida, unlike his predecessor Buhari, is a typical example of a Nigerian mind. He reflects how we think and behave. In Babangida, Nigeria genuinely found a leader they would have normally elected to power. Our duty as a nation is to ensure a genuine transition in thinking to a disciplined and productive mindset, such that the person we would elect to power would be a person like us.

Babangida rode into Nigeria's national consciousness when, almost single-handedly, he put down a coup in February 1976. He rode out of power in August 1993 and went to Minna, Niger State, to enjoy a well-deserved retirement. He has been accused of all kinds of things but not one government after his has been able to go to his Minna home and demand for his arrest. Babangida is nearing his eightieth birthday and presently in ill health. Only posterity can judge him correctly.

CHAPTER SIX

THE NIGERIAN MEDIA

Tunde Oladepo was the Head of Bureau at the Guardian Newspapers' branch in Ogun State. On the 25th of February, 1998, he had come to the Guardian office in Lagos for their monthly board meeting and was determined to make it to Abeokuta that same day to enjoy a relaxed evening with his wife and young children. Due to traffic, Tunde did not make it home until a little after 8pm. The children were just heading off to bed. He took his bath, got something to eat and retired to bed sometimes after 11pm.

At about 3:30am, the Oladepo family were roused from sleep by a loud bang on the gate. "Who could it be…" Tunde's wife said to him. "I cannot tell but let me try and see…" He tried to calm her. With that, Tunde walked into the living room to take a peek at what was happening at his front yard. This part of Abeokuta was not known for robbery; in fact Tunde had specifically sought out this part of town to situate his family because of his infrequent stay outside the home and to ensure that they were safe from robbery attacks.

Just as Tunde was getting to the window to look, he saw gun men jumping the fence of the house and heading towards his house. He rushed and got his wife to stay with the children, while he waited with bated breath for what will follow. With a loud bang on the door, the robbers entered into the house. Tunde approached them nervously, asking what they wanted. None of them spoke to him. The leader of the group approached him and after taking a good look at him turned to his men and said "he is the one".

Without as much as a word of warning, another gunman approached Tunde and shot him point black in the arm, leg and chest. His wife and children let out a scream from within the hide-out where they were. But the gunmen did not bother to go after them; it appeared they had hit their target. Immediately they left the house, leaving behind a bleeding Tunde Oladepo. It was 4:00am in the morning. This was not a robbery; it was a calculated assassination.

After the assassins had left, Tunde's family called out to neighbors to help them. People in the neighborhood converged at the home of the Oladepo's. Tunde was rushed to the hospital but was confirmed dead by the doctors. He had lost too much blood in the space of thirty minute. Tunde Oladepo was dead by 4:30am on the 26th of February, 1998. Many believe that Tunde Oladepo was killed during the murderous campaign of the Sanni Abacha government against journalists and pro-democracy groups during his five year rule from 1993-1998.

The Nigerian media, particularly the print media, decided to wage war with the military regime of Abacha – they did this by wielding the pen against the junta. Numerous articles and news items were published in the print media to embarrass the Abacha government both in the domestic and international spheres. The only way the military government could curb this violence against them was to persecute journalists. A few journalists, like Tunde Oladepo, however paid the ultimate price for this. This chapter shall be examining the story of the Nigerian media and the price that she paid to make the Nigerian nation what she is today.

The Making of the Nigerian Media

The beginning of media activities in Nigeria is closely connected with the coming of Europeans to the shores of this country – particularly the activities of Christian missionaries. The first printing press was established in Nigeria by the Presbyterian Church in 1846 in Calabar. This is clearly some 400 years after the first book was printed in Europe in the late 15th century. In 1859, Rev. Henry Townsend of the Christian Missionary Society (CMS) began the first newspaper in Nigeria.

It was called *"Iwe Iroyin Fun Awon Ara Egba ati Yoruba"* – this can be translated as "A Newspaper for the Egba People and Yorubaland". It should be noted here that the word "Yoruba" was a derogatory term used by the Hausa-Fulani to refer to a group of uncivilized people in the southern parts of Nigeria; whom they called "Yorubawa". But the coming of the newspaper by Townsend help popularize the name "Yoruba" as describing a people from today's Western Nigeria.

In 1937, Nnamdi Azikwe began the West African Pilot. It was a very successful print media outfit that Zik used to publish his political ideas particularly to the people of Lagos and to all of Nigeria in particular. In 1949, Obafemi Awolowo and some Yoruba elite began the Nigerian Tribune. It was based in Ibadan. The Tribune, at first, stood as a reactionary news outlets against the views published by Zik's African Pilot.

The Pilot had gradually become a means of propaganda to advance the political ambition of Nnamdi Azikwe. It was also used as an outlet to publish the successes and advancements of Igbo people living in Lagos. It was said that any Easterner who arrived Nigeria with a foreign degree was published in the newspaper. Awolowo and others realized that if they were going to have a monopoly on the people's minds, they also needed to have their own news medium.

Subsequently, however, the African Pilot and The Tribune found a common enemy: the European colonizers. They gradually reduced the antagonism against each other and rather focused on publishing news and articles that sought to combat the Europeans and spur them towards relinquishing powers to Nigerians – particularly with the growing number of educated Nigerian men and women in society.

It should be noted that between 1859 and 1937 when Zik birth the African Pilot, 51 newspapers had been established in Nigeria. Many of them, unfortunately, were not commercially viable. But this is a testament to the fact that the print media had gained popularity in Nigeria even before the end of the 19th century.

With Nigeria having gained independence in 1960 and the nation gradually slipping into a period of crisis between 1960 and 1967, when the civil war began, the Nigerian media took up another battle. When Kaduna Nzeogwu and his men struck in January 1966, the media carefully followed the story; updating Nigerians on everything that was happening. In fact it was a journalist, Segun Osoba, who would go on to be a Governor in Ogun State, that discovered the body of the Prime Minister Tafawa Balewa, and reported it to the police. This was after days of manhunt to find the missing Nigerian Head of Government.

With the coming of the military, however, the Press took up a new assignment: they sought to press on the military the need to keep their promise of immediate hand-over of power to civilian. In those days when the military came to power, their initial premise for taking over power from a legally elected civilian government was that they were seeking to stabilize the political climate of the country and that they would be returning power to civilians with time.

However with the un-ending military rule of Yakubu Gowon (1966-1974), the media stood as a watch-dog; often reminding the military that their place was in the barracks and not in using the barrel of the gun to coerce Nigerians to submit to them. This often came at a high price as the military and the media continually found themselves clashing and sometimes leading to the incarceration of journalist and even assassination in some extreme cases. The best description of the effort of the Nigerian media to bring sanity to the Nigerian political space is what they did in the days of the Sanni Abacha.

General Sanni Abacha and the Media

When General Ibrahim Babangida (IBB) "stepped aside" in 1993, he left an interim government (ING) in place to rule Nigeria. One of the primary duties of this government was to organize another transition to civilian rule. Having failed twice to transmit powers to civilians, a lot of people did not trust the military any more. The Nigerian media, particularly the print media, were at the forefront of the campaign for Babangida's leaving.

Chief Ernest Shonekan was subsequently made the head of the ING. General Sanni Abacha was made the minister of defense in the ING. Abacha was the only surviving senior officer in the Babangida's government. It is still not clear why Babangida did not retire Abacha. Nevertheless, Babangida left office on the 27th of August, 1993.

A few weeks later, on the 17th of November, 1993, General Abacha toppled the ING and Shonekan was made to leave office quietly. When Abacha rose to power, the first opposition he faced was the Nigerian Media; the press where simply waiting for him. Regardless of what Abacha had to say, the Nigerian Press made it clear she was not going to have anything short of a handing over of power to the rightful winner of the June 12, 1993 elections.

To make matters worse, the winner of the elections, Chief M.K.O Abiola, declared himself President of Nigeria. He was promptly arrested by the Abacha junta and charged with treason. In retaliation, the press came after Abacha's jugular; while he responded with crackdowns on media houses, detention of journalists, seizure of news publications and many other draconian moves as Abacha became increasingly authoritarian.

To ward off critics, Abacha announced a transition to civilian rule on October 1st, 1995. The handover date was expected to be October, 1998. The Abacha junta registered five political parties: United Nigerian Congress Party (UNCP, Congress for National Consensus (CNC), Democratic Party of Nigeria (DPN), Grassroot Democratic Movement (GDM), and the National Center Party of Nigeria (NCPN). Subsequently all five parties adopted General Abacha as their consensus candidate.

The charade was clear to Nigerians. For example the parties were aptly described by Chief Bola Ige as the "five fingers of a leprous hand". Following this, Abacha also turned on his perceived enemies and critics. It is believed that he created some fathom coups for which he implicated a number of high profile critics of his government. They include General Olusegun Obasanjo and General Shehu Yar'adua. Yar'adua did not survive detention; it is believed that he was poisoned. Obasanjo narrowly survived being killed in detention too; someone had warned him not to take a particular drink that was prepared to exterminate him.

In another fathom coup, General Oladipo Diya and some other generals were implicated in a coup. A weeping Diya, clinging to the laps of his boss, Abacha, and begging him to spare his life still remains one of the most unforgettable images that emerged from this period.

Regarding persecution of journalists during Abacha regime Edward Esebonu wrote:

> *"For instance, Godwin Agbroko and Dapo Olorunyomi were detained and beaten with rods and iron batons. Nosa Igiebor and Onome Osifo-Whiskey spent six months in detention. Babafemi Ojudu was detained for eight months without being allowed a change of clothing. Similarly Moshood Fayemiwo, Tony Irolade and Alex Kaba were also arrested and detained at different times, while others like Chris Anyanwu (who lost the use of an eye in detention), Kunle Ajibade, George Mba and Ben Charles Obi were sentenced to years imprisonment by the Abacha junta for involvement in the fantom coup of 1995.[26]"*

The Press however did not go to sleep. As the Abacha government became increasingly hostile, the Nigerian media also began to adopt various means to undermine the Abacha government. One of the things they did was to campaign against the Abacha government overseas. They got their media counterparts in foreign lands to write unfavorable articles against the Abacha government.

For instance the New York Times, The Washington Post and the Washington Times wrote frequent negative articles about the Abacha government. These led to many sanctions imposed on the Nigerian government by world powers; airlines were barred from landing directly in Nigeria – so that if anyone where to fly from the USA to Nigeria, for example, there was no way to get a direct flight; except he transited along the way.

The Nigerian media refused to write anything positive about the Abacha government. Exaggeration and sensational reporting were made against the government. And a high level publication of propaganda in favor of democracy were adopted. The press in the Northern and Southern parts of the country also found themselves

---

[26] Esebonu, E. N. *The Mass Media and the Struggle for Democracy in Africa: The Nigerian Experience*. 2012. Nordic Journal of African Studies. 21(4):183-198. Page 192.

pitched against each other. Papers in the north tended to be more objective and sympathetic to Abacha than their southern counterparts. In the process, the military government bankrolled papers like the New Nigeria and the Daily Times because they wrote favorably about the Abacha government. One report in the Daily Times read:

> *"The principle of patriotism and compassion have been the driving force behind General Abacha's several populist programmes in government. In fact, (Abacha) is the people's general who had always made himself available for national service in moments of travail even at the risk of his life... history bears witness that it was General Abacha's timely intervention in government of the country on 17th November, 1993 that saved the country from disintegration... no other person would have managed Nigeria better...[27]"*

What the Daily Times called a "timely intervention" would have been regarded as a coup in a paper from the Lagos axis. Such was the dichotomy in opinion in the press that the Abacha government created among journalists in this country.

On March 3rd, 1998, in his bid to perpetuate himself in power, Abacha got a number of associations to call for his remaining in power. Rallies were held by Youths Earnestly Ask for Abacha (YEAA) and the National Council of Youth Association in Nigeria (NCYA). These rallies were coordinated by Daniel Kanu and Iliya Ibrahim. They sought to make two million people march on the streets of Abuja, calling for Abacha to remain in power. While all these were going on, Providence had other plans for Nigeria.

On the 8th of June, 1998, General Sanni Abacha suddenly died of a heart failure. It is believed that he died while rendezvousing between two prostitutes of foreign extraction. With his death, the most senior military officer in the military succeeded him. This is how General Abubakar Abdulsalami came to power in Nigeria. He was general

---

[27] Esebonu, E. N. *The Mass Media and the Struggle for Democracy in Africa: The Nigerian Experience.* 2012. Nordic Journal of African Studies. 21(4):183-198. Page 193

known as a non-political soldier. He announced a transition program that would see the military hand-over power to a civilian eleven months from the time of their coming to power. On May 29th, 1999, Chief Olusegun Obasanjo became the President of Nigeria.

The role of the Nigerian media, particularly the Press, in bringing about a change in Nigeria's democratic history has been acknowledged by many. No less than the Nobel Laureate for Literature, Prof. Wole Soyinka, has said that the Nigeria Press is "a hero of Nigeria's democracy"[28].

The Media and Social Responsibility

In the 1940s the founder of Time Magazine, Henry Luce, became concerned with the rising number of totalitarian governments around the world. He and some associates of his felt that a freer Press was the only means of combating the menace. Luce and a few others then came up with a document stating that the media had a social responsibility to society; particularly to combat the rising menace of totalitarian governments.

This was a well thought out initiative because by the 1950s when African countries were gaining independence, almost immediately these governments were being taken over by military regimes. Luce's Social Responsibility was therefore a well-timed initiative that would curb the menace of the military in African and other countries around the world. Edward Esebonu writes on the social responsibility of the Press:

> *"The social responsibility model is based on the idea that media have a moral obligation to society to provide adequate information for citizens to make informed decisions. The main assumption of this perspective is that independent press will serve as a watchdog over societal institutions through objective and accurate*

---

[28] Esebonu, E. N. *The Mass Media and the Struggle for Democracy in Africa: The Nigerian Experience.* 2012. Nordic Journal of African Studies. 21(4):183-198. Page 185.

reportage, and are expected to inform the citizenry of what goes on in the government, which, in a way, keeps rulers in check. In doing so, the mass media will act as the voice of the people, particularly the less privileged. The theory presumes that the practitioners of mass media, by the privilege conferred on them by their profession, should be socially responsible to serve the public interest. This virtue, the theory holds, must be upheld even if it affects profit and antagonizes the interest of the ruling class.[29]"

It is a commitment to this social responsibility that the Nigerian media assumed when it combatted the military and sought at every junction in our national life to ensure that society is properly run by those who have the privilege to be in the ruling class. While it is true that not all media houses have been committed to this principle (many have allowed the pursuit of pecuniary gain to becloud their sense of judgment), the overall majority of those in the media in this country have done their job with the public good at heart.

The New Media: Social Media

The advent of the internet has changed the face of mass media in the world today. Prior to the coming of the social media, people were dependent on print media, radio and television for their news. Before the days of the internet, people usually sought the morning and evening news for a daily dose of information. Others supplemented these with daily newspapers and weekly magazines.

Today, however, the social media has changed the way and manner news reaches the world. When news breaks around the world, social media is available to publicize them almost immediately. Leading social media forums around the world include Twitter, Facebook, WhatsApp, Instagram, and a host of others. In fact social media apps are being

---

[29] Esebonu, E. N. *The Mass Media and the Struggle for Democracy in Africa: The Nigerian Experience.* 2012. Nordic Journal of African Studies. 21(4):183-198. Page 186

developed at almost one per day around the world. The advantage of social media is simply that with an internet on one's electronic device, you are able to get hold of happenings around the world in real time.

Sometimes videos of stories are even published as they are happening. In Nigeria, news sites have become a source of news for many. They specialize in publishing stories on happenings in Nigeria. Nigerians around the World often rely on news sites to get themselves updated about happenings at home.

The trouble with social media as against traditional media however is this: while traditional media houses have a name to protect and therefore are very careful about the stories they publish, this is not so with social media. In social media, any story can be published with little verifiable evidence and such stories could go viral in a very short time. Thus the leading problem of social media is fake news. Therefore those who are intent on getting news updates know that whatever news that one gets off the social media cannot be trusted. So while the news may be going around social media, we wait for more trusted news sites and houses to also publish such stories before believing them.

In recent times in Nigeria, unfortunately, to curb the menace of fake news, the Nigerian legislative house has been pushing for the death penalty against people who publish stories or hate speeches that lead to the death of other persons. Many have kicked against this bill which prescribes the death penalty for hate speech and fake news in Nigeria. People feel that it is akin to using a sledge hammer to kill an ant. Others however think that this is the only means to curb the menace of fake news in the country.

This writer's position is that any law that will discourage irresponsible journalism in the country is welcome. However, it is should be noted that Nigeria's laws already have sufficient edicts to deal with peddlers of fake news. What this country needs is not the making of new laws but the enforcing of existing ones. Also, bringing the death penalty into the matter of the media can be easily be used by a dictatorial leadership to curb the good of social responsibility that the media owes the public.

So that while we may no longer have an Abacha hit squad killing Nigerian journalists around, there could be a leadership in the future that can easily use a law that calls for the death penalty against media men to kill them. We must therefore thread carefully in this matter. The advent of the social media is not a reason to curb the good and responsible work of the media in this country.

CHAPTER SEVEN

CHRISTIANITY IN NIGERIA

I soon die; but I go to heaven! When I reach the gate, angels carry me to the Lord Jesus. When I thank Jesus for his mercy, I come back to the gate and wait there for you. When you come, I not allow angels to carry you – these arms carry you to the Lord Jesus, and I tell him, this is the missionary that preached the gospel to this poor sinner.

– The words (in pidgin English) of a convert on his death-bed in Abeokuta to the missionary through whom he was converted.[30]

If a book will be written on the history of Nigeria, especially as it relates to current happenings in the country and that suggests a way forward for the country, that book must include the story of Christianity on the Nigerian shores. This is the reason for this chapter. In earlier chapters, mention has been made of the coming of Islam to Nigeria.

The Uthman Dan' Fodio Sokoto Islamic Caliphate arose in Northern Nigeria in the late 18th century and then spread to the Eastern parts of the north, although unable to conquer the Borno empire. Efforts were made by Dan' Fodio's jihadist to move south of the country but they were greatly resisted. They were however able to conquer Ilorin and install an Emirate in that town; so that up till this moment, Ilorin is still ruled by a Muslim Emirate.

Christian missionaries, on their part, however, reached Nigeria through the coasts in the southern parts of the country. So that missionary efforts subsequently proceeded from the South right up to the Northern parts of Nigeria. That is why almost two hundred years since Christianity reached the shores of Nigeria, Southern Nigeria still has more Christians in its population than Muslim. This chapter will be examining Christianity in Nigeria. This writer would be looking at how

[30] Abodunde, Ayodeji. *A Heritage of Faith: History of Christianity in Nigeria.* (Pierce Watershed Publishers. Lagos, Nigeria. 2017) Prologue.

much Christianity has contributed to the making of modern Nigeria and sundry matters[31].

Ending Slave Trade

The Portuguese began the business of slave trading in the sixteenth century. In 1526 the first transatlantic shipping of slaves was completed when slaves were taken from the West African coast to Brazil. With the coming of slave trade in Europe also came the rise of evangelical Christianity. Martin Luther began the Protestant movement in 1517 when he pasted 95 theses on the Castle Church in Wittenberg, Germany, challenging scholars to a debate on the biblical legitimacy of the practice of collecting indulgence from the German laity.

After one century, Protestantism had become a thriving religion in Europe; particularly in England where the British monarch had renounced his association with the Papacy in Rome (Italy) and had chosen to form a "Church of England" (Anglicanism) that had the royal head of England also as the head of the Church. In the years between 1730 and 1740, England and the new colonies in what is presently known as the United States of America, experienced what is now called the Great Awakening.

The Great Awakening was a revival of religion that followed the evangelical preaching of George Whitefield and Jonathan Edwards. This revival spurred the consciences of the British people towards the Christian faith and propelled many people to champion social causes that will bring good to their fellow man. In 1765, a man by the name of Granville Sharp began a campaign for the eradication of slavery on the British Isles. He was a Christian and he believed that slavery was man's inhumanity to man.

In 1885, William Wilberforce became a Christian and was convinced that his position in the British parliament ought to be used to better the

---

[31] To write this chapter of this book, this writer is greatly indebted to Ayodeji Abodunde's work titled **A Heritage of Faith: A History of Christianity in Nigeria**. For more information on the history of Christianity in Nigeria, readers are urged to read that book.

lot of the people he represented at Parliament. Granville Sharp met William Wilberforce and the two agreed together to begin to push a bill in parliament that will see to the total abolishing of slavery in the world. It was a tall order at this time since slavery was a source of great revenue for many people both in Britain and around the world but they were convinced that with God's help they would succeed.

Wilberforce introduced the bill to abolish slavery to the British parliament in 1791. He did not succeed in having it passed. But he continued to bring the bill up for argument every year until the 23rd February, 1807, when the bill was finally passed into law and slavery was abolished in Britain and everywhere in the British Empire. It should be noted that it was one thing to introduce a law that abolished slavery, it was however another thing to enforce the law. The British government would subsequently deploy naval manned ships to the Atlantic that arrested any ship carrying slaves and thereafter released those slaves back to Freetown in present day Sierra Leone, where a colony of former freed slaves had been created by the British.

Along with seeing to the abolishing of slavery, William Wilberforce and some friends, that belonged to a group called the Clapham Sect, set up missionary efforts to bring the gospel to Africa. They created the Christian Missionary Society (CMS) that became the leading harbinger of the gospel to the dark continent of Africa in the early 19th century.

Early Missionary Efforts in Nigeria

In 1822 a boy by the name "Ajayi" was rescued by a British naval ship from Portuguese slave traders on the high seas. He was subsequently taken to Sierra Leone where he became exposed to the Christian religion. He would eventually get educated and became an Anglican Missionary to Nigeria. With the settling of slaves from Britain at Sierra Leone, Christianity had become a thriving religion in that West African country. However a series of providential events would occur that would bring the light of the gospel to Nigeria. Ayodeji Abodunde describes what happened:

> *"From 1839, a movement was initiated among the Yorubas in Sierra Leone to return to their homeland. In*

November 1839, twenty-three leading Yoruba merchants in Freetown, including one Nupe and one Hausa man, signed a petition requesting the British government's support for the emigration of their countrymen to Badagry, to start a colony which would be under British jurisdiction. They proposed not only to trade but to also introduce Christianity to their homeland. Their vision was to 'proclaim, in a center of the slave trade over 1000 miles off', a gospel they trusted will sweep away the odious trade: 'that the Queen will graciously sympathize with her humble petitioners to establish a colony to Badagry that the same may be under the Queen's Jurisdiction, and beg of her Royal Majesty to send missionary with us and by so doing the slave trade can be abolished... so that the gospel of Christ can be preached throughout our land.'[32]

Over 500 of these Yoruba men and their families would eventually arrive Nigeria from Sierra Leone. They had been former slaves in Britain but had been come to live in Sierra Leone following the end of Slavery in Britain. They learnt, however, that their roots was in Western Nigeria and thus returned to live closer to their roots. Unfortunately none of them could trace their relatives, so they eventually settled down in Badagry, Lagos.

A missionary by the name Thomas Birch Freeman, was sent by the Methodist Church in Britain to come and work with this group of Christian Yoruba men from Sierra Leone, who had come to Nigeria. Freeman arrived Nigeria in 1842. At first he was with the group at Badagri but he would eventually find his way to Abeokuta, where he went and witnessed to King Sodeke and brought the gospel to that land in December 1842.

After being trained as a minister in England, Samuel Ajayi Crowther was ordained a deacon with the Anglican Church and was sent to Nigeria to work in the budding Christian community that was being set up there. In July, 1846, Ajayi Crowther, Rev. Henry Townsend and

---

[32] Abodunde, Ayodeji. *A Heritage of Faith: History of Christianity in Nigeria.* (Pierce Watershed Publishers. Lagos, Nigeria. 2017). Page 38.

Charles Gollmer, along with their wives, finally arrived in Abeokuta to bring gospel to the Yoruba people.

After sharing their vision with the Egba people, who welcomed them heartily, they got down to work. Providentially, Samuel Ajayi Crowther would unite with his mother and sisters that year, after having been torn apart from each other through slave trade some 25 years earlier. The Methodist Church and Anglican Church would work hand in hand for many years in Yoruba land to establish the gospel in Western Nigeria.

Subsequently, Ajayi Crowther would carry out missions to the Niger Delta areas of Nigeria where he had some great results. Crowther labored on in the Anglican Church until his death in 1891. Bishop Samuel Ajayi Crowther's contribution to early Christianity in Nigeria is immeasurable. He helped to translate the Bible to Yoruba. He was instrumental to bringing education to the people of Southern Nigeria and a host of other things he did in his lifetime.

Rise of Denominations in Nigeria

Up until the early 16th century, Western Christendom had only known one denomination, which was Roman Catholicism. In the 11th century there had been a great schism in Christendom that led to the breaking away of the Eastern Orthodox Church from the Western Church: Roman Catholicism.

While Roman Catholicism was the dominant religion in the Western world – particularly Europe - Protestantism would however splinter Christendom further in Europe, so that by the end of the 30 Year War in 1648, Europe had come to terms with a new concept in Christianity: denominationalism. Denomination is the idea in Christendom that while Christians are largely agreed on the Bible being the word of God, certain groups of Christians allow for certain doctrines and practices to be peculiar to them. Bruch Shelley writes on Denominationalism:

> *"Denominationalism, as originally designed, is the opposite of sectarianism. A sect claims the authority of Christ for itself alone. It believes that it is the true body*

> *of Christ; all truth belongs to it and to no other religion. So by definition a sect is exclusive. The word denomination by contrast was an inclusive term. It implied that the Christian group called or denominated by a particular name was but one member of a larger group, the church, to which all denominations belong[33].*

To therefore avoid continual conflict in church life, denominations were allowed to exist. Therefore when Nigeria came under Western Christian influence denominationalism also came with. Thankfully many of the early missionaries, particularly the Protestant ones, played down the denominational differences between them; but those differences existed all the same.

Mention has been made of the coming of a Methodist minister to Badagry in 1842 by the name Thomas Birch Freeman. His missions in Badagri did not take on a "Methodist" outlook. He rather focused on bringing the gospel to a people without God and without Christ. Later in 1845, he was joined by the Rev. Henry Townsend, a missionary sent by the CMS. The CMS had an Anglican bent to their missions but they also did not emphasize denominational differences. Townsend would subsequently proceed to Abeokuta, along with Samuel AJayi Crowther, to establish a Christian mission in that town. This was in 1846.

Between 1850 and 1852, there was a need for a military invasion of Lagos. The king of Lagos then, King Kosoko, was still dealing in slaves. The missionaries in Badagri were unhappy about this and they knew that this would inhibit their efforts to reach Nigeria with the gospel – considering also that slavery had been abolished in Britain at that time. In 1851, a detachment of British forces arrived Lagos and deposed Kosoko. A new king, Akintoye, was installed. Subsequently a missionary by the name James White was sent by the CMS to Lagos to bring the gospel to bear on that city.

A missionary by the name of Hope Masterton Waddel was sent by the Scottish Presbyterian Church to Calabar to bring the gospel to that town in April 1846. Waddel was quite a committed Presbyterian and very focused at establishing this denomination in Calabar town. It was

---

[33] Shelley, Bruce. *Church History in Plain Language*. (Thomas Nelson Publishers. Nashville, Tennessee. Fourth edition. 2013). Page 318.

the Scottish Presbyterian mission board that would eventually send Mary Slessor to Calabar in 1876.

Baptist Missions to Nigeria began in 1850 through the efforts of Thomas Jefferson Bowen. When Bowen arrived Nigeria, he spent some time with Rev. Townsend in Abeokuta, learning the Yoruba language and culture. He would eventually proceed to Ilorin with the hope of establishing the gospel in that city. He however did not find the people of Ilorin receptive to the gospel. Subsequently he relocated to Ogbomoso.

The king of Ogbomoso was very welcoming and Bowen would eventually establish a mission in that town that would bring Baptist Christianity to Nigeria. In the year 1853, emigrants from Brazil and Cuba brought Roman Catholicism to Lagos. When the Catholic Church in Europe realized that there was a rising number of Catholics in Nigeria, they decided to send Catechists and Priests to Catholic devotees in Lagos. Seventh Day Adventists pioneered a work in Nigeria in 1914. It was begun by a man called D. C. Babcock in a small town called Erunmu, a little distance from Ibadan.

In 1900, following a conference of Christian leaders in Edinburgh, UK, the need to reach the interior parts of Africa became very paramount. The Sudan United Missions, which would eventually be named the Sudan Interior Missions (SIM), was set up to reach unreached areas in the inner parts of the African continent. The SIM was not denominational in outlook. They were rather focused at engaging Muslim tribes all around the interior parts of Africa. This mission group, which is still very functional in Nigeria today, were the first to take the gospel to cities in Northern Nigeria.

Pentecostalism and Charismatics in Nigeria

In the year 1900 a man by the name of Charles Parham in the United States of America claimed that he and his followers had received baptism in the Holy Spirit and now possessed the ability to speak in tongues. Prior to this incident, much of Christendom regarded this phenomenon as having ceased to exist. Christians still remain largely divided over whether or not people can speak in tongues today.

In Nigeria, at St. Paul's Church, an Anglican assembly, led by the Reverend James Johnson, in 1916, the Pentecostal phenomenon had also taken root. Reverend Johnson held the opinion that Pentecostalism was a biblical experience for Christians today. He urged his parishioners to pursue it.

In the 1930s, an evangelist with the Apostolic Church in Nigeria, Ayo Babalola, began to carry out preaching and healing services all around South-west Nigeria. These phenomenon sparked people's interest in the matter of the charismata in Nigeria's Christendom. It is said that Babalola's revivals were so exceptional that even the white missionaries who witnessed them were dumb-founded. In the mid 1930s, Augustus Wogu began Pentecostal and Charismatic meetings in South-East Nigeria. His ministry in these areas is what brought about the Assemblies of God's churches to Nigeria.

At the height of the Apostle Ayo Babalola's revival, a Pentecostal missionary by the name Sidney G. Elton arrived Nigeria in 1937. Elton was also awed by the healing and miracles that he witnessed, he however positioned himself to give the revival a theological garb by guiding all who were involved in it to see it from a biblical point of view. In those days when such revivals broke out, extremes were easily introduced into it. But with Elton's influence, the leaders of the revival were properly guided. S. G. Elton had a fruitful ministry in Nigeria until his death in 1987.

In 1952, a man by the name of Josiah Akindayomi left a Cherubim and Seraphim (C&S) church to pursue a call to ministry that he believed God had placed on him. Akindayomi had been pastoring a local C & S church in Lagos and had developed a reputation for holding prayer meetings that helped people find solutions to problems in their lives.

When he left the church, he started an assembly called *"Ijo Ogo Oluwa"*[34]. Later that year, the name of the Church was changed "Ijo Irapada" or "The Redeemed Church". This church would gradually jettison much of the C & S practices and take up more Pentecostal and Charismatic outlook in its doctrines. At his death in the early 1970s, a little known Pastor E. A. Adeboye succeeded Afikundayomi as pastor and overseer of this church. This church is today known as the Redeemed Christian

---

[34] Translated "Church of the Glory of God" in English.

Church of God (RCCG). It is believed to be the largest Pentecostal denomination in Nigeria today.

Following the Nigerian civil war and the destruction and trauma that this event had on the psyche of many Nigerians, especially on those from Eastern Nigeria, the tendency to turn religion to a means of solving human problems, rather than it being God's method of converting sinners, started to creep on Nigerian Christianity. This gradual decline was slow but steady. By the close of the 1970s, a new kind of Christianity had invaded Nigeria. It was a Christianity that sought to use faith in God to get the good things out of life. Welcome the Prosperity Gospel.

The Gospel of Prosperity

Following the Nigerian civil war that ended in 1970, one man came to the Nigerian Christian scene and changed it forever. His name is Benson Idahosa. Idahosa had had a sudden conversion in the early 1960s. By the end of that decade he had begun to have evangelistic crusades all around the country. He would later meet with missionary S. G. Elton who introduced him to Gordon Lindsay, an American and the foremost World Evangelist of that era.

After a brief stint at Lindsay's Bible School in Dallas, Idahosa dropped out and returned to Nigeria with a strong burden to evangelize the country. Idahosa also started a church in Benin, Church of God Mission International, which had hundreds of branches around Nigeria. He had a Bible School that trained pastors in the ministry. But most of all, he took the country by storm with his electric preaching style and evangelistic prowess. He was also often guest to foreign Pentecostal/Charismatic churches in the United States of America.

In 1978, Pope John Paul II decided to ordain some Pentecostals as Archbishops, in recognition of the rising influence of Charismatic theology and practices around the world. The Roman Catholic Pope ordained Benson Idahosa the Archbishop of Pentecostalism in Africa. From that point on, it appears that Idahosa's ministry and spiritual life took a downturn. He became increasingly ostentatious in dressing and grandiloquent in his speech. He adopted the Prosperity Gospel that was becoming increasingly accepted in the United States.

Even S. G. Elton who had ordained him to ministry, protested his new manner of doing ministry and decided to dissociate himself from Idahosa's ministry. By this time it was too late. Other pastors who looked up to Idahosa had adopted the prosperity theology and had begun to preach it also.

So that from the 1980s up to this present moment, the gospel of Prosperity has become a vital theology in Pentecostal and Charismatic churches. The likes of E. A. Adeboye, David Oyedepo and even conservative preachers like W. F. Kumuyi now preach full blown Prosperity Gospel. These men have trained thousands of other ministers in Nigerian Christendom and they all preach the same thing in their churches.

The gospel of Prosperity is a departure from the orthodox Christian message because besides teaching that Christ died to redeem sinners from their sins, the prosperity gospel also teaches that Christ was seeking to make people healthy and wealthy. The prosperity message was not preached by any missionary that came to Nigeria.

It was developed as an answer to the trauma of a country just recovering from a civil war, and a country that was at the mercy of bad leaders who had very little initiative to improve its economy. While the prosperity gospel was being heralded everywhere in the country, another phenomenon was brewing in the background that would knock Christians back to their senses: it is the coming of Boko Haram to the Nigerian scene.

Boko Haram

Islam has always had a radical dimension to it. Prophet Muhammed, the harbinger of the religion, employed wars, what they prefer to call Jihad, to propagate his doctrine in and around Mecca in present day Saudi Arabia. While those wars were of necessity because Muhammed and his followers were forced to defend themselves against their persecutors, Islam has since employed Jihad to spread its religion all around the world.

Most of the Middle East, where Islam is today predominant, where countries where Christianity was once practiced. But Islam took over many of these regions with the force of arms. Even when Uthman Dan' Fodio began his propagation of the Muslim religion, he employed the force of arms to spread his doctrines to many parts of Nigeria.

So when, in 2009, Muhammad Yusuf, a young man in Borno State, began to teach radical concepts of Islam. Teaching also that western education and western civilization should be forbidden (or Haram), and was doing this with the threat of violence, he was not especially doing something novel. Yusuf saw examples in many historic Muslim movements and he understood that a secular society, run by today's government, given to Nigeria by the Western world, was his biggest enemy.

He thus declared Western civilization haram or "Boko Haram" and from this the group got their name. It was not long before this group clashed with Nigeria's security agencies and full blown violence was unleashed on the police and the people of Maiduguri, Borno State. Muhammed Yusuf was arrested by the police and executed extra judicially in 2009. Many of his followers who survived that clampdown have since gone underground and are now utilizing guerilla warfare to actualize their goal of setting up an Islamic caliphate in northern Nigeria.

While Christians in Southern Nigeria were basking in a new found revelation that God desires that they are healthy and wealthy, the task of taking the gospel to unreached areas in northern Nigeria was left undone. These areas that are some of the poorest parts of the country became a hot-bed for radical Islamization of young minds.

This is the making of Boko Haram. The solution to the problem however must be two fold. First there must be a successful military decapitation of the group. This is to be followed by proper educating of the young people of this region of the country. And as this is happening, Christians must move into all unreached areas in Northern Nigeria with the gospel that is able to save sinners from their sins.

Modern Christian Reactions

In 2017, an On-Air-Personality with Cool FM, Lagos, who bears the moniker "Daddy Freeze" began a campaign against tithing in churches. His argument was this: tithing was an Old Testament injunction given to Jews and Christians were not obligated to tithe. While many may have been championing this view long before Freeze came to the scene, it was after he made his position known via his social media handle on Instagram, that the matter became a national debate.

Churches became very disturbed by this position and quite a number of leading pastors in Nigeria, including E. A. Adeboye and Johnson Suleiman, came out to condemn Daddy Freeze's position on tithing. But what they said did not deter many church goers. In no time, churches began to witness a fall in their revenue and many of them began to update their members on the need to give to church faithfully.

The Daddy Freeze reaction against tithing was coming in the backdrop of thirty years of the prosperity gospel in many Charismatic Churches in Nigeria. Besides promising adherents a life of ease and plenty, the prosperity preacher also taught members that the only way to enter this league of wealth is to give and to give sacrificially. So that for a long time, Christian ministers, particularly those of the Pentecostal/Charismatic extraction, had lived large off the largesse of ordinary people in churches.

Many of them becoming stupendously rich, affording to buy mansions, private planes and numerous cars. Their children were also going to the most expensive schools, within and outside the country. A generation of young people therefore grew up in church witnessing these obscene display of wealth by pastors within an economy that was becoming increasing hostile to the average Nigerian. Daddy Freeze and others only reacted to this situation and the reactions have led to many other forms. Today young people are not only ceasing to tithe to churches, many are dropping out of churches altogether. Others are renouncing religion; taken up atheism as their personal worldview.

To conclude this chapter, it should be noted that the development of Christianity in Nigeria is the story of the modern Nigerian state. Britain who colonized Nigeria was a Christian nation and therefore imposed a Christian worldview into our national life. It should also be noted that while the modern Nigerian state began to take shape from 1900, Christianity had begun to thrive in Nigeria since the 1850s.

Despite the spread of Christianity in Nigeria, the heart of the Christian message has been lost over the decades in this country. The first missionaries were primarily concerned with helping the locals understand the gospel and come to living faith in Christ Jesus. Unfortunately a generation of missionaries came that became preoccupied with establishing denominational boundaries in the country.

This was followed by the rise of the Pentecostal and Charismatic movement. The Prosperity Gospel these churches brought with them has cast Christianity in a bad light in the country and Christians would be using the next few decades to clearly distinguish the gospel of Christ from that of prosperity. In all of these the message of the gospel continues to ring in Nigeria; calling all men to forsake a life of sin and believe in Christ.

CHAPTER EIGHT

1999: NIGERIA RETURNS TO CIVIL RULE

Nigeria's Nobel Laureate and Africa's first Nobel Prize winner tells the story of how he learnt of General Sani Abacha's death in his Memoirs: *You Must Set Forth at Dawn*. Soyinka had been one of the leading thorns in the flesh of the Nigerian maximum ruler. He had gone into exile sometimes in 1995 when it became obvious to him and all around him that to continue to confront a totalitarian Head of State like Abacha within the shores of Nigeria was to seal one's sure death. 1995 was also the year the Abacha government executed Ken Saro-Wiwa and his other Ogoni comrades. That action sent a clear signal to all that were fighting Abacha: this man could do anything, including fighting dirty.

Soyinka's travel papers and passports had been seized by a judiciary that was playing to the tune of Abacha. But in the most clandestine manner and one that would go down in world record as one of the greatest escapes in world history, Wole Soyinka stole out of Nigeria through one of our porous borders on the outskirts of Saki, Oyo State. Immediately he arrived in the United Kingdom, he joined forces with other pro-democracy activists and they began an outright attack on the Abacha government. Soyinka and others were the brains behind *Radio Kudirat*. This was a communication outfit that beamed radio signals into Nigeria from an unknown destination.

They used this channel to sensitize the Nigerian public against the despotic rule of Sani Abacha. Every effort that the Nigerian government sought to shut down this radio station failed.

Sometimes in early 1998, it became obvious to Soyinka that both radio broadcasting and other pro-democracy campaigns were not going to change the mind of Abacha. This man was ready to perpetuate himself in office by all means. Soyinka decided that guerilla warfare was the final solution. He got in touch with his eldest son, Olaokun, and told him he was returning to Nigeria. Olaokun enquired why. Soyinka responded that he was going to be taking arms against the Nigerian government. Olaokun, a medical doctor, said he also would be returning to the country with his father. Soyinka could not convince his son not to come.

Before making the trip back to Nigeria, and having gotten good supplies of arms ready to be shipped to the borders of Nigeria, from where they would launch the attack on Abacha, Soyinka decided to visit Israel. He had finished dinner one particular night and then took a stroll into the nearby hills. He was watching the stars and gazing at the beauty of nature. Of course, his dear country Nigeria was uppermost in his mind. That night he knew instinctively that the decision to return to Nigeria and fight for her liberation was the right one. He returned to his hotel and was heading to his room to sleep, when he got the message: Abacha, the Nigerian despot, was dead.

General Abubakar Abdulsalami

No one knows exactly how General Sani Abacha died. Some of the more reliable account has it that he had flown in Indian prostitutes and was in the middle of a sex orgy with them, when his heart failed and he died suddenly in between two of them. While this story may be disputed, what was known to many Nigerians was that Abacha's health was failing. Sani Abacha lived a certain life of debauchery and this included heavy drinking.

Newspapers around the country had gotten wind of his medical report that showed that the Nigerian Head of State was in the final stages of liver cirrhosis. This was understandably denied by the people in government but not a few people knew that his days on earth were numbered. Despite his failing health, Abacha still had time to exert his weak body to wild sex. His heart failure was a natural consequence.

At the time of his death, the person that wielded the most power in government was a man called Major Hamza Al-Mustapha. Al-Mustapha was Abacha's chief security man. He was also alleged to have been the brain behind the killer squad that the Abacha government ran to silence opposition. Al-Mustapha claimed that Abacha died in his hands and he had the powers to take over government at that point. However, military hierarchy demanded that the most senior officer becomes head of state at the demise of a military head of state. The most senior officer at the time of Abacha's death was General Abdulsalami Abubakar.

General Abubakar was born in 1942 in Minna, Niger State. He is first cousin to General Ibrahim Babangida. Unlike Babangida, however, he was a professional soldier and not a political one. He stuck to his duties within the military and seldom took up political appointment – like many soldiers did in those days because it afforded them the opportunity to enrich themselves. He was one of those soldiers who had always advocated the return of the military to the barracks. He was not liked by Abacha and rumour had it that Abacha was planning to retire him when death suddenly struck. Abubakar became the Nigerian Head of State a day after Abacha died - the 9th of June, 1998. Immediately he announced that his government would be using less than a year in power before they hand over to a democratically elected government.

General Abubakar immediately set the machinery in place for a quick hand over of power to civilians. He created the Independent National Electoral Commission (INEC). He saw to the redrafting of the 1979 constitution and approved it as the constitution of the Nigerian state in 1999. He spent his time in office laying the groundwork for a successful handover of power to civilians. He was clearly intent on ensuring that power will get into the hands of the right person and for this reason he visited even persons like Wole Soyinka in their hide-out in the United Kingdom and invited them to run for the Presidency. Soyinka turned the offer down; stating that he did not see himself as the President of Nigeria.

One stain on the Abubakar government was the death of Moshood Kashimawo Abiola in detention during his tenure. Many had advocated the position that with the death of Abacha, Abiola would automatically become the President of Nigeria. Talks were still ongoing on the matter when Abiola was reported to have died in his detention cell on 7th of July, 1998 – about a month after Abacha's death. Some claim he was poisoned. Abiola died exactly two days to the day he was to be released from detention.

When Abdulsalami received the news of his death, he immediately telephoned Emeka Anyaoku, an elder statesman and one who had acted as a bridge between the military and civilians even while Abacha was alive. Anyaoku immediately instructed that an autopsy be performed on Abiola's body but that it must be done by two separate teams of pathologists from the USA and Britain – since Nigerians were likely not to trust our local pathologists. The autopsies were done and the result indicated that Abiola died of natural causes: a heart attack. It is believed that the excitement of his coming release from detention may have precipitated a heart condition that led to his death.

Thereafter, Abubakar released all political detainees that the Abacha government had slammed in jail. This included Chief Olusegun Obasanjo. Obasanjo was later approached by his friends to run for the presidency of the country. After an initial hesitation, Obasanjo took up the challenge and ran on the platform of the People Democratic Party (PDP). Obasanjo tells the story of how his children reacted when he informed them he was going to run for the Presidency:

> *"My mind was almost made up, but I had to consult with my children. I got four of them together in New York. I told them I was about to decide whether to go into politics or not. Iyabo was the most antagonistic. She burst out loudly, 'I know you will join and you will die there and if you die, I will not weep.' I told her 'if I die and you weep, it is for yourself and others, not for me as I would not know you are weeping.'... It was only Segun who gave me a few words of encouragement by saying, 'Daddy, you have always said that we must serve God and humanity and if this is the way you have chosen to serve God and humanity, I will pray for you.' With all these the die was cast.[35]"*

---

[35] Obasanjo, Olusegun. *My Watch.* (Okadabooks.) Volume 2.

Suffice to say that Obasanjo eventually decided on going into politics full time and he made a success of his time there.

The 1999 Elections

On the 20th of July, 1999, General Abubkukar Abdulsalami abolished the five parties that had been created by the Sani Abacha regime. These five parties had already adopted Abacha as sole candidate, with elections slated for August, 1998. Unfortunately, the despot did not live to see the contraptions he had put together come to fruition.

In its place, the Abdulsalami regime instituted a transition program that was to culminate with the military handing over power to civilians in May 1999. This step taken by the Abdulasalmi regime was a brave one, considering the fact that in 1979 some senior military officers had complained that Obasanjo's hurried transfer of power to civilians, laid the foundation for the shoddy civilian government of Shagari that succeeded them. Despite this criticism, Abdulsalami was still intent on handing over power to civilians at the most, one year after his coming to office. He did everything humanly possible to set the stage for a successful transfer of power to civilians.

When Professor Wole Soyinka turned down his offer to run for Presidency, Abdulsalami turned to Chief Olusegun Obasanjo for help. Obasanjo had been locked up in Yola prisons by the Abacha government on trumped up charges of planning a coup to overthrow his government. Abdulsalami released Obasanjo a few days after Abacha's death. Even while he was in prison, Obasanjo was being besieged by visitors; many of them pressing on him to run for presidency. Obasanjo was tired and poor. The Abacha government had nearly bankrupted his farm while he was in prison.

He also needed to pay attention to his health. Leading a country was not a top priority for him at this point in time. When he was released from prison, one of the first things Obasanjo did was to write to the widow of Sani Abacha and to express his condolences at the passing of her husband. It was a considerate thing to do; particularly to show that he had no ill feelings towards Abacha or any member of his family.

When Obasanjo returned to his home country in Otta, Ogun State, he was visited by former Head of State General Ibrahim Babangida. Obasanjo had been one of Babangida's harshest critics while he was in government. Yet, Babangida visited him and pleaded with him to come and lead Nigeria. After due consultations with his family and some friends, Obasanjo gave in.

Obasanjo joined the People's Democratic Party (PDP) on the 28th of October, 1998. He chose PDP because, of all the parties in those days, this was the only party that had a truly national appeal. All the others seem to have had a regional appeal like the parties of the days of the past. In the PDP, there were Nigerians of various extractions. It also had a strong military presence with no less than forty retired senior military officers as members. The PDP convention held in February 1999. Obasanjo beat Chief Alex Ekwueme with 1,658 votes, while the Ekwueme could only poll 521 votes. After the convention and primaries, Obasanjo chose Alhaji Atiku Abubakar to be his running mate. Abubakar had won the election to be the Governor of Adamawa State but he relinquished the position to be running mate to Obasanjo.

Atiku was also the successor to General Shehu Yar'Adua who had been Obasanjo's deputy in 1979 but who had died in detention under the Abacha regime. Obasanjo chose Atiku to compensate the Yar'Adua group that worked frantically for his emergence at the primaries. Elections held that same month of February and Obasanjo was elected President of Nigeria on the 27th of February, 1999. Obasanjo defeated Chief Olufalae of the AD by polling 63% of the total votes casted in the elections. Yet, Obasanjo did not win one single state in the South West were he hailed from. The Yoruba people voted massively for Chief Olu Falae. Richarch Bourne states the factors that made the choice of Obasanjo as President of Nigeria a good one:

> *"There are three elements: the choice of a tough personality, Obasanjo, to be the first president in Nigeria's third republic; the creation of a nationwide party, the PDP, as a vehicle for managing a polity that can sometimes seem ungovernable; and the philosophy of a pacted transition, which involved a compromise between rival beneficiaries of the military regime and their democratic opponents.[36]"*

All of these factors and a whole lot others played out for an advantage to bring Obasanjo to power again, having been military head of state from 1976 to 1979. In 1979, when Obasanjo was leaving office the man who led the military march past was a young Lt. Col. Abubakar Abdulsalami. Providence would have it that the same Abdulsalami led the military to hand over power to a civilian government to be led by President Olusegun Obasanjo.

Factors behind Nigeria's Successful Civilian Governments from 1999

Before the year 1999, Nigeria had never had a successful hand over of power from one civilian government to another. In 1964, the Balewa government had only entered its second term in office when it was overthrown by a military government. In 1983, the Shehu Shagari government had also only entered its second term in office, when it was ousted out of office by Major General Muhammadu Buhari and others.

So it was as if it was impossible for Nigerian politicians to hand over power to each other. However, on May 29th, 2007, Chief Olusegun Obasanjo completed two terms in office and handed over power to Alhaji Musa Yar'Adua – a two term governor of Katsina State and the younger brother of late General Shehu Yar'Adua. The jinx of an unsuccessful civilian-to-civilian transfer of power was broken. Since 2007, Nigerian politicians have successfully handed power to each other on two other occasions: 2011 and 2015. The following are factors that have contributed to a successful civilian to civilian transfer of powers.

Relocating Nigeria's Seat of Power:

Nigeria witnessed her bloodiest coup ever when Gideon Orkar and a few other young military officers invaded Dodan Barracks on April 22,

---

36 Bourne, Richard. *NIGERIA: A New History of a Turbulent Century*. (ZED Books Limited, London, United Kingdom. 2015). Page 203.

1990. The mutineers sought to lay their hands on General Babangida but at the very last moment, just before they broke into his room, Babangida was whisked out of Dodan Barracks and taken to a secret hideout in Surulere – all of these in Lagos.

After the coup plotters were arrested and investigations into the coup was conducted, it was revealed that one of the problems with frequent coup plots in the country was the porous nature of the country's seat of power which was at Dodan Barracks, Obalende, Lagos. So following the coup, Babangida doubled up efforts to ensure that the nation's capital city was taken to Abuja.

In Abuja, the office and residence of the nation's head of state was to be situated on a large piece of land called Aso Rock. It was planted on top of a hill with large vegetation and forests surrounding it. Besides the electric fencing of the whole perimeter of the Aso Rock Hill, the nation's seat of power is largely impregnable. Security is at its optimum at Aso Rock, so much that since the country's capital had moved to Abuja there has not been a coup; except the palace coup conducted by Sani Abacha that removed Ernest Shonekan as head of the Interim Government that Babangida had put in place when he left office.

Military Government Becoming Increasingly Unpopular:

While military takeover of government was quite rampant in newly independent countries in Africa in the 1960s, by the 1990s military governments were becoming increasingly unpopular. Western nations, on which most African countries found sustenance, made it clear to African rulers that democracy needed to thrive on the continent. For this reason, any military government that came to power by force of arms was treated like a pariah nation. Sanctions were placed generously on such governments and the world would not associate with them until they returned powers to civilians.

So military takeover of government was no longer seen by soldiers as a welcome idea because if they were to do it, they would be so unpopular. Gradually military coups have become almost non-existent in Africa today.

-**Nigeria's developing democracy**: By far, the greatest factor to sustainable democracy in Nigeria has been Nigeria's own developing democratic ethos. The simple fact is that Nigerians have learnt from the mistakes of the past and are bent on ensuring a better future for themselves and their children. While democracy is not the only system of government in the world today, it is by far the most popular and the most workable.

Gone are the days when monarchs ruled the land; Nigeria is today a republic – a state that is ruled by democratic principles. Like a baby learning to crawl, Nigerians have worked on their democracy and we are a lot better than when we started. Indeed we have a long way to go, but the fact remains that if this country can reach the point that she is today, she can become a strong democratic nation in the days to come.

1999 was the year that democracy took its roots in Nigeria. Many individuals can be named who contributed to the success of the country's democracy so far, but by far it is the people of this nation that must be praised for remaining dogged and committed at making the nation work. All Nigerians, both those in the diaspora and at home, have put their hands together to make the country work. The country has survived a civil war. We have survived years of military rule. We have survived autocratic governments. And by all means Nigeria will survive all other ills that will befall her on the path to becoming a nation to be reckoned with among the committee of nations.

CHAPTER NINE

2015: DEFEATING AN INCUMBENT

On May 29th, 2007, former Governor of Katsina State, Alhaji Musa Yar'Adua was inaugurated as the President of Nigeria. He ran on the platform of the People's Democratic Party (PDP) and had received the blessings of President Olusegun Obasanjo to succeed him in office. Yar'Adua had everything going for him. His two terms as Governor of Katsina, from 1999 to 2007, had been largely successful. This northern state enjoyed the concentrated commitment of democratic dividends such that it made large strides forward under Yar'Adua's rule.

So his success as a state governor commended him to the electorate as one who was likely to succeed as President. Yar'Adua was also from an aristocratic family in Katsina. His father had been a popular politician in the first republic. His brother, Shehu, was Obasanjo's deputy in the army and had been some sort of a martyr under the Abacha government. Musa Yar'Adua also came to power commending himself to the Nigerian people as one who was committed to development and democracy. He is the first graduate of a tertiary institution to rule Nigeria. One of the first things he told Nigerians, in his inaugural speech, was that the elections that brought him to power were flawed and that he was committed to ensuring better electoral processes in the future. Yar'Adua had invited Goodluck Jonathan to be his running mate, in the run-up to the 2007 presidential elections. Jonathan had just been installed as Governor of Bayelsa State, after his principal, Chief

D.S.P Alamieyeseigha, was removed from office when he was convicted of corruption charges.

One thing however that was against Yar'Adua was his health. It was quite obvious to Nigerians that we had a sick president in our hands. While the Presidential campaigns of 2007 were on, Yar'Adua was alleged to have collapsed. While the PDP made very little of the incident, Nigerians were worried because Yar'Adua had to be flown abroad for medical treatment. To allay the fears of Nigerians, President Olusegun Obasanjo, who was campaigning actively for Yar'Adua, called him from a campaign ground and that was the scene where Obasanjo said on the phone "Umoru, Umoru, are you dead?...". It was one of the high points of the 2007 elections.

Of course, a dead man would not be able answer. But an obvious alive and well Yar'Adua responded that he was not dead but alive. The Yar'adua administration began on a full throttle. It is to his credit that the Niger Delta disturbances were brought to much abeyance. Yar'Adua suggested an amnesty program for former militants in the creeks of the Niger Delta. He made it clear to them that the government understood their agitation and he was committed to bringing development to the Niger Delta. Under him, the Niger Delta Development Commission (NDDC) went into full swing.

The Niger Delta people, rather than continue in violence, decided to throw in the towel and accepted the government offer of amnesty. Thousands of young men laid down their arms and took advantage of the government's offer to rehabilitate them. The NDDC also sent hundreds of these young men for training at home and abroad to rehabilitate them. President Musa Yar'Adua was in the second year of his administration when his health began to fail. The trouble with this matter was that the people around him did not want Jonathan, a Southerner and a Niger Deltan, to succeed Yar'Adua; so everything was done to keep the state of health of the President under wraps.

Yar'Adua would eventually be flown abroad, sometimes towards the end of 2009; yet Jonathan was not installed as acting President. It was about this time the word "cabal" came into the Nigerian political lexicon. The late Dr. Dora Akunyili had protested publicly that a "cabal" had taken over the running of government, while Yar'Adua was incapacitated health wise.

Doctrine of Necessity

In January 2010, Pastor Tunde Bakare, Professor Wole Soyinka and some other prominent Nigerians began a protest walk in Lagos under the auspices of the Save Nigeria Group (SNG). Their main campaign was that since the President of Nigeria, Musa Yar'Adua, was likely ill and incapacitated, and could not formaly transfer powers to his deputy, Goodluck Jonathan, the National Assembly should step in and declare Jonathan the acting President of Nigeria.

The SNG protests were timely because while Yar'Adua was ill, the allegation that a group of people who were not empowered by the Nigerian constitution were running the country, was unfortunately true. A lot of things was left undone and it appeared that the ship of state was just sailing aimlessly. Some people even alleged that the President's wife, Turai Yar'Adua, was the one running the country and directing the Armed Forces in her husband's absence.

It was so bad; no one was sure where the President was receiving treatment. None of his close political associates could see him. The Nigerian Senate, headed by David Mark, was also in a fix. There was no law in the Nigerian constitution that said the National Assembly could empower the Vice President to become Acting President. But there is such a thing as a "Doctrine of Necessity". Wikipedia defines a doctrine of necessity thus:

> *"The doctrine of necessity is the basis on which extra-legal action by state actors, which are designed to restore order, are found to be constitutional. It also includes the ability of a private person to violate a law without punishment where the violation of law was necessary to prevent even worse harm. The maxim on which the doctrine is based originated in the writings of the medieval jurist Henry de Bracton, and similar justification for this kind of extra-legal action have been advanced by more recent legal authorities, including William Blackstone[37]."*

---

[37] Wikipedia. *Doctrine of Necessity.* www.wikipedia.org/wiki/Doctrine_of_necessity. (Accessed on 13th December, 2019)

On the 10th of February, 2010, the two arms of the National Assembly, the Senate and the House of Representatives, passed a resolution, which they jointly termed a "Doctrine of Necessity." There they stated that since the President of the country was not in a position to empower his deputy to act as President, they as lawmakers in the Country, have hereby empowered Goodluck Jonathan to be the Acting President. With this, Jonathan came to be the first Head of State in Nigeria, from the South-South of Nigeria. He was fully empowered, according to the constitution of the country, to act as the President of the country – though in an acting capacity but with the full authority of a President.

On the 5th of May, 2010, news reached Nigerians that President Musa Yar'Adua had died. He did not survive his ailment. Until his death, no one was really sure what he had been suffering from. He was buried in his home state of Katsina. That very day, the Chief Justice of Nigeria swore-in Goodluck Jonathan as President of Nigeria. It was a bitter-sweet experience for Nigerians. First, we had lost a Head of State. But secondly, someone from a minority tribe in Nigeria, Ijaw, and from the South South, was now President of Nigeria.

Muhammadu Buhari

Muhammadu Buhari was the Head of State of Nigeria, from December 1983 till his overthrow from government in August, 1985. For close to three years, he was detained by Ibrahim Babangida. When he would eventually be released, he returned to his home town of Daura in Katsina State, but his family life had been infiltrated. Apparently while he was incarcerated, Babangida had extended help to Buhari's wife and children. When Buhari returned home, he was unhappy with this development. The crisis led to the breaking up of his marriage with his first wife. Buhari would eventually get married to a much younger woman, Aisha, who many claim was a good friend to his late daughter, Zulaihat. Buhari laid low throughout the administration of Babangida. When Babangida "stepped aside", General Sani Abacha invited Buhari to come and lead the Petroleum Trust Fund (PTF). Nigeria had been making some extra funds from the sales of oil that was not in the budget.

The Abacha government decided to save up this money in a fund that was to be administered by the PTF. Abacha was convinced that Buhari was the best man for the job. Much of the testimony that proceeded from the work of the PTF shows that Buhari managed these funds very well; although he was alleged to have given priority to northern states and their institutions.

In 2003, Muhammadu Buhari contested election to be President of Nigeria. He ran under the platform of the ANPP. At this time, Obasanjo was seeking a second term in office. At the polls, Buhari got 11 million votes, while Obasanjo had 24 million votes. Buhari disputed this election and took the result to the court. He was however unlucky as the Supreme Court ruled against him.

In 2007, he would again run on the platform of the ANPP and challenged Yar'Adua at the polls. Yar'Adua and Buhari were from the same home state of Katsina. Yar'Adua defeated Buhari at the polls and the old general was forced to seek his mandate in another election. In 2010, Buhari fell out with his party, ANPP, and decided to create another party called the Congress for Progressive Change (CPC). The CPC was formed in 2010; just a few months to the general elections of April 2011. Buhari took an unprecedented step in this election. He chose Pastor Tunde Bakare as his running mate for this election.

He said he had observed Bakare lead the protest with the Save Nigeria Group (SNG) and felt that this was the sort of man that he could work with. They led a vigorous campaign and sort people's hands in the elections. Their biggest opponent was Goodluck Jonathan of the PDP. Jonathan was the incumbent President and he had all the financial war chest to win the elections. A few weeks to the elections, it became clear to the Action Congress of Nigeria (ACN), the party that Asiwaju Bola Ahmed Tinubu was leading, that they could not win the elections without entering some alliance with Buhari.

They therefore sought Buhari for an alliance but it failed because the terms of the alliance, which was offered to Pastor Bakare, was not suitable to him. When the country went for the April 2011 elections, Buhari was again roundly defeated at the polls by the incumbent Goodluck Jonathan. Jonathan polled 22 million votes to Buhari's 12 million. Some parts of northern Nigeria, where Buhari enjoyed much popularity, were plunged in violence.

That year, 2011, INEC had just begun to use members of the National Youth Service Corp (NYSC) for the elections. Some youths in the north therefore blamed the outcome of the results on these corp members and attacked them. About twelve corp members were killed. Many blamed Buhari for these outbreaks of violence because he had made some utterances that could incite violence in the public.

When Buhari failed at the polls in 2011, he vowed he would be retiring from politics and would not seek elective office again. In fact, he made a tearful video where he explained that he had sought the office of the presidency three times and it had remained elusive to him. At this time, some Nigerians were beginning to have some sympathy for him. After the elections, the chieftains of the ACN approached Buhari and members of the CPC for a coalition. The process towards coming together to become a mega party would eventually play out as an advantage for Buhari and others. Other factors will also work in their favor.

Build Up To The 2015 Elections

It did not take very long for people to realize that Goodluck Jonathan was not a very capable leader. By the end of 2010, after holding the reigns of powers for a few months, it became clear to people observing the nation's politics that Jonathan was not in charge of his government. In fact many people alleged that his wife, Patience, who was very much a semi-illiterate, had greater hold of his government than he did.

Yet, Jonathan enjoyed the sentiment that he was from the Niger Delta, the oil producing section of the country, and that "their son" deserved a time in power. On January 1st, 2012, the Goodluck Jonathan administration decided to hike the price of fuel. A coalition of civil society groups came together, at the Gani Fawehinmi Freedom Park, to protest this hike in fuel price. The protest went on for two week and greatly embarrassed the Jonathan administration. Jonathan would eventually be forced to roll out soldiers to curtail the protest. Fuel price was reduced but the Jonathan government was beginning to lose popularity.

In April 2012, a detachment of Boko Haram fighters invaded a sleepy

Borno community called Chibok and carted away no less than 200 girls that were writing their final secondary school examinations. In spite of the security in that part of the country and the fact that schools had been warned to close down, these girls were all taken away into the stronghold of the terrorists.

These events plunged the country into an uproar. The Jonathan government was labeled clueless. A group of Nigerians began the "Bring Back Our Girls" campaign and in a little while the whole world had keyed into it; with the wife of the former American President, Barack Obama, Mitchelle, also joining the campaign – holding a card asking for the girls to be returned. Till the time of this writing, some of these girls remain with the terrorist group - **Boko Haram**.

As all these were going on, allegations of corruption began to be bandied around top officials of the Jonathan government. The Minister for Petroleum, Mrs. Deizani Allison-Madueke, was said to have mismanaged billions of dollars; while stories made the rounds of her family members and associates reeling in stolen wealth.

The allegations of corruption was so much that Jonathan was asked on live TV what he understood corruption to be. His response "stealing is not corruption" will again hunt his administration as one that did not have the good of Nigerians at heart. Thus the twin evils of corruption and violence were working against the Jonathan government, when the country approached the 2015 elections.

Besides the troubles that Jonathan was having, the opposition which Buhari and Tinubu led was building up a mega party to remove power from the hands of Jonathan and the PDP. On the 6th of February, 2013, a coalition of parties came together to form the All Progressive Congress (APC). The major parties that came together were the Action Congress of Nigeria (ACN), the Congress for Progressive Change (CPC), ANPP, and the All Progressive Grand Alliance (APGA). There were other splint groups even from the PDP, with persons like Bukola Saraki and Rotimi Amaechi, who were former governors of Kwara and Rivers States respectively, leading their supporters to the APC.

Besides the coming together of these political warlords, a campaign of calumny against Jonathan began on social media. While the social media had existed since 2007, Nigeria felt the weight of its influence on our politics the most in 2015. All kinds of information, true and false, were being propagated against Jonathan on Whatsapp, Facebook, Twitter and other social media platforms.

The Jonathan administration also continued to feed their enemies things to make fun of them with. the *"dia ris God"* statement that Mrs. Patience Jonathan made at the wake of the capturing of the Chibok girls. This was used against the Jonathan administration to paint them as an uneducated lot. All of these were happening as the country was drawing near to another general elections in 2015.

In February 2015, when the elections were to hold, the Jonathan administration decided to postpone the elections for another six weeks. They claimed that INEC was ill prepared. People believed that this was done to postpone the evil day. Buhari defeated Atiku at the APC primaries to become presidential candidate for the party. By the time the elections would hold on the 29th of March, 2015, Jonathan was as good as gone. The incumbent president polled a mere 12 million votes at the polls, while Buhari had 15 million votes. The whole country went into a jubilant mood. It had never happened before that an incumbent would defeated in an election in this country.

To the credit of Goodluck Jonathan, he did a lot to allow for a level playing field for the emergence of his opponent. Jonathan was often quoted to have said that his ambition in politics was not worth the blood of any Nigerian. In fact, he said the following about the violence that engulfed the country after the 2011 elections:

> *"One of the most traumatizing moments of my presidency was the cold blooded murders of youth corpers in the north following our victory in 2011. I thought long and hard over the waste. It just did not make any sense. How does a parent lose everything like this? How does a nation kill its future in this manner? I still recall the spread of their names in the papers. The promise of a close tomorrow. They were graduates already. Almost all of them from the South and one of them from North Central... Kogi[38]".*

---

[38] Jonathan, Goodluck. *My Transition Hours*. (LWCA Publishers. Nigeria. 2015). Page 11

The INEC Chairman, Prof. Athahiru Jega, was almost done with announcing the result of the elections. Nigerians had gone into a jubilant mood. No one was sure if Jonathan would accept the result of the elections. In fact, one of his supporters, Godswill Orubebe, had invaded the collation center in Abuja and insisted that the results of the elections were to cease being called out.

Some reports had it that America and Great Britain had begun to warn their citizens of impending violence in Nigeria. All of a sudden, the media began to report that Jonathan had called Buhari to congratulate him on winning the elections. Jonathan was reported to have said that he wished Buhari the best and even invited him to the State House to discuss the modalities for a proper and peaceful transfer of power.

While Goodluck Jonathan may not have done everything right when he was in power, by peacefully relinquishing power when he lost the 2015 election – he demonstrated that he was a man of peace and whatever he may have done in government, Nigerians were ready to forgive him. He has since returned to his hometown of Otuoke, Bayelsa State, to enjoy a well-deserved retirement.

So Far With Buhari

It has been observed by many that no other person came into power in Nigeria with as much goodwill as President Muhammadu Buhari. Because Goodluck Jonathan had become quite unpopular, the popular mantra during the election that saw him exit power was *"anything but Jonathan"*. Jonathan was depicted as a leader under whom corruption was rife and who had no idea how to curtail the violence in the North East parts of the country. But Buhari, who was a former military man, had the credentials of one who could deal with the Boko Haram menace. He was also known as incorruptible person. So there was indeed massive support for his presidency.

However, after four year of being in power, Buhari seems to have squandered some of the goodwill that brought him to power. While the kind of corruption and violence that were witnessed under the Jonathan Presidency have subsided (not totally eliminated), the Buhari administration has been bedeviled with its own peculiar problems.

There is the challenge of Buhari's nepotism: his penchant to favor people of northern extraction and to put only northerners in office. In 2015, prior to Buhari appointing ministers, the only people that were appointed to head government establishments were mostly northerners. Today, a northerner is the Head of Government, Head of the National Assembly, and the predominant heads of the security agencies. Most recently, and particularly after his winning a second term in office in 2019, Buhari has been replacing almost everyone whom he appointed that were of non-northern origin with northerners.

The real trouble with Muhammadu Buhari's leadership is the problem with every northern leadership: fascism. Prior to the coming of the Europeans, the North had been ruled by a strong fascist system. There are usually a string of Emirs that rule the people. Therefore, there is always the rulers and the ruled in the Hausa/Fulani society. The people therefore exercise a mentality of "these are the big men" and *"we are their subjects"*.

Most northerners who are born with a ruler mentality, always believe they are born to rule. While those who are born with the subject mentality, never aspire to any great height in life. This is why northerners never protest any kind of fascist government over them. On the other hand, southerners do not have this mindset.

They understand that if every man works hard enough and is smart enough, he can be anything he wants to be in life. Southerners will therefore not accept any kind of leadership over them that may wish to undermine them. This is the reason why most of those who protest bad governance come from the south of Nigeria; while northerners are forever subservient to any kind of leadership that is held by them — whether it is a military or civilian government.

It hasn't been all minuses with the Buhari administration. There are a couple of pluses. Buhari's government seems to be making giant strides in the areas of infrastructural development and the anti-graft war. Some examples are the revitalization of the railways and the successful prosecution of senior members of the ruling party for graft (Senators Orji Uzor Kalu, Joshua Dariye, and Former Governor Jolly Nyame), who are currently serving time in prison.

A Reason to Rejoice

The defeat of Goodluck Jonathan still remains a great feat in this country's history and it is a testimony to the fact that our democracy is making progress. This is a reason to rejoice indeed. One only needs to remind oneself of where this country is coming from. We are coming from an age when the British made one set of people, the northerners, believe they are far better than others and that the right to rule this country belongs to them.

We have since moved from this through an oppressive military regime until we got to the point of almost having a one party system, when the PDP said they would rule Nigeria for sixty years. Right before our eyes, with a unified mindset, Nigerians removed an incumbent from office and put their choice. The good news is that because the people of this nation have done it once, they sure can do it again. What is abundantly clear is that when the people of this country will go to the polls in 2023, they would be a lot wiser.

As the country makes progress in appointing leaders at the federal level, a revolution has also been taking place in the appointment of governors, senators, and members of the federal house of representatives. The story of Oyo State, in the 2019 elections is a case in point. It saw a people elect a PDP man, Seyi Makinde, in a region that was dominated by APC stalwarts – the South West of Nigeria. These are the progresses we are seeing and with a much more improved political environment, the Nigeria people are bound to enjoy more and more of the dividends of democracy they have fought so hard to obtain.

CHAPTER TEN

THE PRIVATE SECTOR AND EMERGING POSSIBILITIES

Ever since Nigeria discovered oil, the country has been largely dependent on foreign exchange obtained from sales of this product to foreign countries. Oil revenue makes up more than 60% of the nation's gross earnings. In recent times, however, it has become very clear to observers that the world is moving away from the use of petroleum products because of their adverse effect on the environment.

Nigeria has also seen that if its economy will thrive in the years to come, it would have to look to other means of making money. To be able to do this, the private sector of the country must come alive. Professor Yemi Osinbajo, Nigeria's Vice-President, shared similar sentiments while inspecting the LADOL shipyard installations in Lagos in August 2018. He said:

> *"The Nigerian economy has to be private sector led, this project is an example. A $16 billion project, in naira terms that is around N5 trillion, the entire Nigerian budget is N9 trillion which is the highest in Nigeria's history, spending on infrastructure is N1.5 trillion and it tells you that (this) single project is more than the entire Nigerian budget for infrastructure excluding state budgets and this is the story of developed economies in the world.[39]"*

The LADOL shipyard is a private initiative in Lagos that houses the Egina Floating Production Storage and Offloading (FPSO) installations. It is the first fully fabricated and integrated FPSO in Nigeria. Yet this company is investing N5 trillion into one project in Nigeria. This is an example of what is happening in the private sector in Nigeria. In this sector, there are lots of emerging possibilities and it has been suggested by many that this is the sector of Nigeria that will save the country at last.

In this chapter, we would be examining a number of private sector institutions in Nigeria and we would be concluding with a thought on the emerging possibilities they are bringing; especially opportunities for young Nigerians both to invest in, and to find jobs within. We should note that it is not possible to treat every private sector entity available in the country because in an emerging economy, these opportunities keep increasing by the day.

Telecommunications in Nigeria

Prior to the coming of mobile phones to Nigeria, the country had operated a vast network of telephone communication that was run by state owned NITEL – Nigerian Telecommunications Limited. It was during Olusegun Obasanjo's first term in office (2000) that mobile phones became common use in Africa; in fact Nigeria was one of the last countries to plug into the mobile telephony revolution.

The Obasanjo government would eventually grant mobile operational license to three companies: MTN, Econet and Globacom. Globacom (or glo) was an indigenous company owned by the business Tycoon, Mike Adenuga. With the coming of the mobile phones, popularly referred to as GSM – Global System of Mobile Communication, there was a revolution in this private sector of business in Nigeria. Job opportunities opened up first for Engineering graduates from Nigerian universities, such that the oil companies were not the only places where these young graduates were going to get jobs.

---

[39] Fadipe, Olumide. 2018. 'Nigeria: Why Nigeria's Economic Revival Must Be Private Sector Driven – Osinbajo'. *AllAfrica*. 11th August, 2018. Accessed: 16th December, 2019. www.allafrica.com/stories/201808110011.html...

A lot of Nigerian graduates with Engineering degrees were the pioneer staff for these companies between the years 2000 and 2005. There were also subsidiary job opportunities for marketers, who sold recharge cards to people. Today, the mobile telephone aspect of Nigerian telecommunications offers an array of vast business opportunities for Nigerians in various fields of life. Nigeria is the largest market for mobile phones in Africa today.

There are those who deal basically in sales of phone accessories and many other phone related business opportunities. In Lagos, there is a market called "Computer Village" in Ikeja. In this place, all kinds of phones, computers, and other electronics are sold. It is a multi-billion dollar market and it began to flourish mainly after the mobile phone revolution in Nigeria. Besides the Computer Village, each town in Nigeria has a marketing center where phones and their accessories are sold.

The coming of mobile phone telephony to Nigeria's private sector has opened up the private sector in Nigeria; it has allowed for hundreds of young Nigerians to become successful entrepreneurs. It has opened up job opportunities for many Nigerian graduates. And it continues to be a point of reference of what successful private sector in a country can be.

Banking

The Banking sector has been another aspect of the private sector in Nigeria that has helped the country to grow and to offer jobs to a lot of Nigerians. The first bank to begin functioning in Nigeria is the African Banking Corporation, which is today known as First Bank of Nigeria. It started operation in the country in 1892. Following this, other banks like Barclays Bank of Nigeria, United Bank for Africa (UBA), and the African Continental Bank, all commenced activities in the country during the colonial era.

The Nigeria banking sector took up new life following the Charles Soludo led banking sector reforms of 2004. Charles Soludo, as Governor of the Central Bank of Nigeria, which is the arm of government regulating banking activities in the country, gave directives that all banks were to shore up their capital base from N2 billion to N25 billion. This led to a number of banks coming together in a coalition. Others sought partnership with foreign banks. But the result was that the banking sector in the country possessed a solid capital base for foreigners to come into the country and invest.

Throughout the years, while government had sought to provide jobs for the teaming unemployed youths in Nigeria, the banking sector in the country became a sought of refuge for many seeking jobs. In fact, it became some sort of a platitude for many young Nigerians to say that if one could not get a job anywhere else, you could as well settle for a bank job. While the banking jobs were easier to get, they were quite rigorous to function in. Nigeria banks, in a bid to shore up their capital base and to compete in the very competitive environment that the CBN had created for them, usually resorted to sharp practices to function.

Young ladies were often employed in this sector to bring in investors to the bank by any means possible – so that it became quite common for young girls to sell their bodies to get potential investors in banks. Bank employees were also often weighed down with outrageous targets that they were urged to meet. Which made many of these employees to do anything possible to get potential investors. Besides the sharp practices, though, the Nigerian banking sector has grown greatly. It has strengthened the private sector arm of our national life and it continues to be one of the leading employers of labor for many unemployed youths in the country.

Entertainment

The Nigerian entertainment scene has provided a great deal of opening for young and entrepreneurial Nigerians to develop their talents and make good money in the process. Entertainment in the country began with many Nigerians cutting their teeth in music. The likes of I.K. Dairo, Kayode Fashola, King Sunny Ade, Onyeka Onwenu, and the recent ones like Timaya, Tuface Idibia, Dbanj, Wizkid and Davido, have taken Nigerian music, both traditional and hip-hop, to the African continent and even worldwide. At the time of this writing, Burna Boy, a Nigerian musician, has been nominated for the 2020 Grammy

Awards. More and more, Nigeria music is being recognized at the international stage.

Right on the heels of the music industry is Nigeria's movie industry. Popularly called "Nollywood" (patterned after Hollywood in the United States of America), Nigeria's movie industry has made great progress since its inception in the 1960's. The Guardian reports:

> *"(The Nigerian movie industry is) worth over USD5 billion and producing more films than Hollywood. Nollywood is today the second-largest movie industry in the world by volume after Bollywood and contributes 5% to Nigeria's GDP. It is also the second-largest employer in the country, proving its huge socio-economic impact. Through Nollywood movies, Nigerians have been able to influence viewers worldwide and export the 'Nigerianess' of their culture, their lifestyle and even their accent.*[40]*"*

Nigerian movies are seen in every country in Africa, with the ones exported to francophone countries subtitled in French. This has opened the movie industry in the country affording for movie makers to invest more and more in movies. In recent times, a lot of criticism has followed the making of Nigerian movies and some innovations have been brought into the making of our movies.

So that in 2018, Genevieve Nnaji produced the movie "Lionheart". It was internationally acclaimed and even submitted to the Academy Awards to be nominated under international movie categories. Unfortunately it was disqualified on very controversial grounds. It is believed that with time Nigerian movies will begin to compete with those made in the United States of America. One particular challenge that has bedeviled Nigerian movies is our movie maker's inability to invest the kind of money into movies that would make them compete with their international counterparts. It is believed that if the Nigerian government will invest in movie making in this country, Nigeria would

---

[40] Editor. 2018. 'Entertainment Industry, a vital piece of Nigeria's economic puzzle'. The Guardian. 4th September, 2018. Accessed: 18th December, 2019. www.guardian.ng/news/entertainment-industry-a-vital-piece-of-nigerias-economic-puzzle/

be on the verge of taking over movie making in the world.

The rise of Nigerian music, movies and other entertainment arms in the country has opened up channels for young and talented Nigerians to be very productive and to be able to make a great deal of money from foreign exportation of their intellectual property. This is another way the Nigerian private sector is thriving independent of government.

Sports

Nigeria's first appearance at the Olympics games was in 1952. In 1954, Emmanuel Ifeajuna won gold in high jump at the Commonwealth Games in Cardiff, United Kingdom. Incidentally, the same Ifeajuna would join the Nigerian Army, rise to the rank of a senior officer, and partake in the first military coup of 1966. The Nigerian Football League began in 1972 with five teams. This would later grow to 12 teams in 1978. Today, there are at least two leagues that coordinate football activities in the country.

In 1985, the Nigerian Under-17 Youth Team won the maiden edition of the World Cup in faraway China. Nigeria has gone on to dominate football in Africa having won the African Cup of Nations in 1980, 1994 and 2014. In professional Boxing, Nigeria has produced World Champions: Hogan "Kid" Bassey, Dick Tiger, and Bash Alli. In December 2019, Anthony Joshua, a Nigerian born British Heavyweight boxer, reclaimed his title from Mexican, Andy Ruiz, after he had lost it to him in June 2019.

At some point when it seemed the Nigerian political climate would refuse to take-off, the Nigerian name and undying spirit was kept afloat by the successes of our young men and women in international sporting events. Nigeria has thrived in the Olympic, Commonwealth Games, and many other sporting events. The Nigerian can-do spirit has been clearly exemplified in the efforts of our young people as they have made a mark for themselves in sporting events abroad. Thankfully, while many nationals are known to stow-away while on sporting duties at international events, very few Nigerians have been recorded to have done this. Our young men and women continue to make us proud in sporting events around the world. Although, some of them have had to change nationalities to those of other countries for economic reasons – understandably.

Oil and Gas

Nigeria is the highest oil and gas producer in Africa. Nigeria's oil reserves is estimated to be between 16 and 22 billion barrels. Some estimates claims that this could be as much as 35.3 billion barrels. While oil exploration had existed in Nigeria since the 1900's, commercial production of oil did not begin until the 1950's. Since oil is the major foreign exchange earner for the country, the sector is largely regulated by the Nigerian government through the Nigerian National Petroleum Corporation (NNPC).

Nevertheless, oil explorations are not carried out by the Nigerian government but rather by licensed private companies. The first company to begin oil exploration in Nigeria was the Shell Petroleum Development Company (SPDC). After the coming on of SPDC, other companies have joined the exploration of oil in the country. They include: Mobil, Chevron, Agip, and Elf. While all of these companies are foreign companies, they do indeed employ Nigerian nationals to help run their companies. Therefore, working in oil companies has become the leading lucrative job in Nigeria. And to be fair to these companies, quite a number of Nigerians have been employed in these companies which provides them a source of livelihood.

In September 2013, Aliko Dangote announced to the Nigerian public that he had secured $3.3 billion as an initial deposit to finance the construction of an oil refinery in Lekki, Lagos. Prior to this time, Nigeria has not been able to refine enough crude to meet the demand for fuel in the country. The three refineries built by the country in the 1970's are largely moribund. Therefore, while the nation is an oil producing country, we depend on foreign countries to refine the crude we use in our vehicles. This has created a huge market for Premium Motor Spirit in the country and thus necessitated a great need for a private entity to refine our oil within the country itself.

Dangote simply latched on this need and his refinery is almost nearing completion. This refinery will be processing at the least 650,000 barrels of crude oil every day. At full production it would be processing 50,000,000 litres of gasoline every day. This amount is estimated to meet a great demand for fuel in the country and reduce our dependence on importation of fuel.

The good news about the Dangote refinery is that it would offer thousands of job opportunities to Nigerians, again increasing the private sector capacity in the country. It is believed that after Dangote has commenced work, the oil and gas sector would be opened up to more Nigerians. It would reduce Nigeria's dependence on government for jobs and it would bring greater prosperity to the average Nigerian family.

Transportation

Due to the large population of the country, Nigeria's transportation business is big business. It is a private sector in the nation's labor market that employs quite a huge amount of man-power. Unfortunately, most of those who are engaged in this sector, especially those driving on highways, are usually uneducated. This has therefore cast a negative slur on the transportation business in the country. In spite of this, those who have invested in transport in Nigeria have always ended up smiling to the bank.

Nigeria has the largest road network in West Africa. She also has the second largest road network south of the Sahara with roughly 108,000 km of roads. The challenge the nation has had however has not been in building more roads but in maintaining existing ones. This is the reason why the transportation sector, as lucrative as it is, still remains greatly challenged. Bad roads tends to damage vehicles and they are the leading source of motor accidents in the country. Government after government have sought to correct this perennial problem of bad roads but it still remains a leading problem in the country's transportation system.

Besides roads, other means of transportation will include air, rail, and waterways. Nigerian railways used to be very efficient up till the 1980's. Afterwards, the rail system has been largely moribund. The Obasanjo administration sought to revamp the Nigerian Railways. A lot of money was invested in revamping the rails and new trains were purchased. Yet, the rail system remained moribund.

The Buhari administration has however revamped the rail system in most parts of the country. About a year after the Buhari government came to power, Rotimi Amaechi, Minister for Transportation, completed the rail lines between Kaduna and Abuja. State-of-the art trains were installed and this means of transportation has become the preferred means for many Nigerians who live or do business up north, especially with the rising cases of armed banditry and kidnapping along the Kaduna/Abuja expressway.

While Nigerian Airways is today comatose, air transportation still remains big business in the country because there are private entities that continue to invest in it. And since our roads are not safe, many Nigerians still prefer to use air to reach their destinations. This has made travelling by air very popular among Nigerians. Nigeria's transportation sector is one of the leading employers of labor in the country. It is also a sector that has strengthened the private sector of the country. A lot more can be gotten from the transportation system in the country if the government would be committed to regulating this sector for optimal performance. One of the ways they can do this is to ensure that basic infrastructure like power and roads are in good condition.

Manufacturing

Another aspect of Nigeria's private sector that enjoys the advantage of a large population that Nigeria has, is the manufacturing sector. With a population of almost 200 million people as at 2019, if one were to produce a good or service today, you are bound to find at least 1,000 people you can sell it to and earn a profit in the process. On this basis and even on a larger scale, the manufacturing sector of Nigeria has thrived.

Goods ranging from cement, food and beverages, tobacco, textile, wood production, chemical and pharmaceuticals, plastic and rubber materials, electrical and electronic appliances, iron and steel, and motor vehicle parts, are some of the products that are produced in the country. Nigeria remains a viable environment for manufactured products. The high income that the country earned from foreign exchange in its sale of oil to western countries made Nigeria a viable place to set up manufacturing plants in the 1970/80's.

When corruption however set in, the manufacturing companies also began to suffer because rather the people stealing the countries monies to invest further in the country, they were taking them outside the country and making credit facilities available to other manufacturing outfits in other nations; while Nigerian manufacturers were lacking credit and were unable to produce as they normally should. Another problem that hit the manufacturing sector was the failing power supply that the country began to witness following the nation's civil war.

At some point the cost of producing goods and services was becoming too expensive because manufacturing plants would require fuel for their generators – which then hiked the cost of producing those goods. With time, many companies began to shut down and move to neighboring countries like Ghana to produce their products. In the process, Nigerian professionals and artisans were losing their jobs.

In spite of the gloom, many manufacturing companies continue to do business in Nigeria and thrive. The cost of production has only made the cost of products higher. Government also realizes the importance of keeping manufacturing companies in the economy; thus, they ensure that credit facilities are easily accessible for them. Many waivers are provided for those importing raw materials into the country. And government continues to ensure that these companies have security and some basic infrastructure to enable them do their business here. As manufacturing companies thrive, jobs are available for Nigerians in the private sector and the economy of the nation thrives as well.

Emerging Opportunities in Nigeria

The main purpose of this chapter is to shift the focus of the reader from the government to what other sectors of the country are doing. One of the leading problems in Nigeria is unemployment but it may not necessarily be that there are no jobs, but that young graduates are looking in the wrong places.

For example, if a graduate were to leave school today, the first place they look at for jobs is in the oil and gas sector, and then maybe manufacturing, before settling down for government jobs – which turns out to be the most sought after because in Nigeria, government remains the highest employer of labor. The focus therefore of the concluding section of this chapter would be to help readers see emerging possibilities in the Nigerian labor market and to help our teeming unemployed youths to engage themselves in this sector.

There is a concept called "Glocalization[41]". It is a hybrid of a word combining "globalization" and "local" together. It simply means that it is possible for one to be doing an international job right in one's local environment. The implication is that the person would be employed by a foreign organization, paid (mostly) in dollars, and would be operating from his local base right here in Nigeria.

There are hundreds of international bodies looking for able and smart Nigerians that would carry out assignments for them here in the country. Most of the time, one does not even need to meet the employers. You simply communicate through the internet. This is one reason why ability to use the internet is a must for every millennial today. After such jobs are delivered, you get paid and move on to other assignments.

The main reason why Nigerians are failing to get glocalized jobs is because many Nigerians are not honest individuals. Many people are seeking to get rich quick and do not present an honest wage to their employers. This way they lose out on such jobs. But if one is skilled at what he/she does and is honest, the person would put himself in a position to be entrusted with assignments for which he would be well paid.

What this translates to is this: Nigerians must begin to be skilled at what they do. The attitude that our undergraduates have in which they only read-to-pass must stop. Such behaviors may earn them a good grade in school but it would not give you the required skills in your profession. Our young graduates must begin to learn to hone their skills and become truly proficient in their field of study.

––––––––––––––––––––––––––

[41] I heard the term "Glocalization" from a seminar conducted by Bayo Adeyinka, a blogger and banker, in Ibadan in 2019.

There is a cankerworm eating into the life of young graduates, particularly the Christian ones, who spend all their waking hours in fellowship in the university. They leave school and go away with a false notion that they have been called by God to open churches and become General Overseers. This cankerworm is destroying the professional life of young graduates. Our undergraduates must realize that they are in school to learn a skill and not learn religion. If after they have gotten a skill and have made a success in their field of calling, they now branch off to missionary endeavors, they would look more honorable and not seem like persons who have had to resort to religion when they could not make it in normal life.

With skill and sincerity, job opening would come to one in various ways. Most of the time, it would come where one is originally working. This is why the best place to look for a job is within the very place you are right now. Do your job well and you would be recommended by others. It is through such recommendations that international jobs come and one is right on his way to glocalization.

It is important that Nigeria gets this matter of work right or else the country is heading into a bleak future. We have all the advantages. We have a large workforce that comes from a large population. We are a nation with a lot of resources. There are many opportunities in Nigeria that naturally would not open up in foreign countries. Nigeria is still largely unregulated so the usual bottlenecks that one would encounter in other countries are not here. This is where one can truly make it if one would put his/her mind in honest work. The future of this country is bright and our young people can make a success of this country, regardless of what the fathers have done in the past.

CHAPTER ELEVEN

GREAT NIGERIANS

Under the government of Umaru Yar'Adua, Mrs. Dora Akunyili was made Minister of Information. She felt that one of the leading things she needed to do during her tenure was to rebrand Nigeria. As she pursued this mission, she crafted the slogan that Nigerians are a "Good People, Great Nation". As good as this might sound, the average Nigerian mentality wholly swallowed Mrs. Akunyili's optimism in a flood of pessimism. Nigerians were not convinced that this country was a great nation and they did not think they themselves were good people. Nigeria had developed a reputation in foreign countries for advanced fee fraud, they said for example.

We were competing with Jamaicans in the United States for every kind of crime imaginable. Dora Akunyili, on the other hand, felt that if the image of the country could be rebranded, a new lease of life can emerge from the country and further impact the people of the country positively. Nigeria could have a better image outside, she argued.

The truth of the matter is that while Dora Akunyili's efforts were commendable, Nigeria did not need "rebranding" in the strict sense. While the image of a nation can be affected by the nefarious actions of a few people, at the same time the good works of other people is also sufficient to put a positive mark on the way other nationals see that country. In fact, what the country needs is not a lot of people doing a lot of good or pursuing some rebranding efforts, what Nigeria needs is to shed light on the works of a few good Nigerians. And already this is happening.

Nigeria is indeed a great nation. The greatness of the country has been eclipsed by generations of bad leadership but this has not stopped the greatness of the country from coming forth. In fact, the hope of a

Nigeria that would emerge in the comity of nations as a great country rests on a few good Nigerians. This chapter would be spending time to examine ten great Nigerians[42] and their contributions to the good of humanity, both from within the shores of Nigeria and outside the country.

1. Agbani Darego

Agbani Darego was born in Lagos on the 22nd of December, 1982. Two years later, her family relocated to Rivers State where they hail from. She is the sixth child of eight children which her parents had. At the age of twelve, while away in boarding school, Agbani's mother succumbed to her battle with breast cancer. It was a tragedy that would eventually shape the whole psychology of the family, particularly those of teenage Agbani Darego.

Probably to overcome the loss of a mother and the loneliness that comes with it, Agbani took an interest in modeling and believed that someday she could contest in a beauty pageant. Her father did not share her enthusiasm. Mr. Darego is Roman Catholic and a conservative, like most African men of his generation, and was not enthusiastic about putting his children in the spotlight of entertainment and bliss.

Somehow, however, father and daughter reached a truce. If Abgani would take up a career in modeling she was not going to do it like the women of her time: "...you will not be wearing all those revealing clothes and so on...," her father insisted. Agbani agreed to her father's rules and thus entered into the world of show business.

In 2001, Agbani Darego entered the Most Beautiful Girl in Nigeria (MBGN) pageant that is organized by the Silverbird Group owned by Senator Ben Murray Bruce. To the astonishment of everyone, Agbani was crowned the winner of the competition. The reason why this was surprising was that Darego was not fair skinned and she did not make any effort to bleach. She won the beauty pageant despite her dark complexion.

---

[42] Note that the arrangement of their names here is not in any particular order.

That same year, Agbani entered the Miss Universe competition and became the first Nigerian to make it to the top ten semi-finalist. In keeping with her promise to her father, she wore a modest maillot rather than a revealing swimsuit like other contestants did. In November of 2001, she went on to win the Miss World beauty pageant. This feat was what published her to the whole and she suddenly became a national hero in Nigeria.

Today, Agbani Darego is married to Ishaya Danjuma, the son of Billionaire former army general - Gen. Theophilus Danjuma (rtd). They have a son together, who was born to them in September, 2018. Agbani Darego has continued to spread the great Nigerian brand through her numerous modeling work. Although today, she lives quietly with her family in New York, she continues to represent the can-do spirit of an ordinary Nigerian who can rise against all odds within the country to become an international figure. The story of Agbani Darego is the success story of a Nigerian committed to make it with the blessing of Providence.

2. Philip Emeagwali

Philip Emeagwali was only thirteen years old when the Nigerian civil war broke out in 1967. Being someone from Eastern Nigeria, and considering the mass exodus of Igbo people back to the East, after Col. Ojukwu had said he could not guarantee the safety of any Igbo man living outside the perimeter of the then Biafran nation, the Emeagwali family were compelled to leave Akure, where Philip had been born in 1954, and head home. When Philip arrived Enugu, the Biafran nation was at a feverish height to enter into war with their Nigerian brothers.

Besides the shortage of ammunition to wage the war, there was also a shortage of man-power. So when some Biafran warlords approached Philip's father to ask him to allow his thirteen year old son join the Biafran army, Mr. Emeagwali had little choice. This was how young Philip was conscripted into the Biafran army.

While Philip embarked on a few expeditions at war, he was fortunate to return alive and was never sent to more perilous battle fronts. His superiors soon recognized that young Philip's gifting was not in handling machine guns but intellectual. He would therefore spend more time as secretary to his Biafran battle units and as an errand boy. Besides, he was also too young for the violence of war.

Philip was already sixteen years old when the war came to an abrupt end in January, 1970. He immediately concluded his secondary school education and as he concluded a correspondence course with the University of London in the early 1970s, he won a scholarship to study Mathematics at Oregon State University in 1977. He would later bag a Master degree in Ocean and Marine Engineering from the George Washington University. Then he got another Masters in Applied Mathematics from the University of Maryland. He would later obtain a doctorate in Civil Engineering from the University of Michigan. His thesis was actually on scientific computing.

Philip Emeagwali is one of the few people that brought such innovations to the world of computers that we can now boast of "supercomputing" in the world today. An association of computer scientist of Africans in diaspora wrote of Philip Emeagwali on their webpage:

> *"Philip Emeagwali's greatest achievement, that warranted him the most praise, was The Connection Machine. The Connection Machine utilizes 65,000 computers linked in parallel to form the fastest computer on earth. This computer can perform 3.1 billion calculations per second. This is faster than the theoretical top speed of the Cray Supercomputer. Though he did not invent The Supercomputer, his work on it won Philip Emeagwali the Gordon Bell Prize in 1989. The parallel computer was twice as fast as the previous year's computer. The Connection Computer was a great advancement over previous designs built by IBM's design team of Thomas J. Watson Jr. and Fred Brook.[43]"*

For his work, even Bill Clinton cited him as an example of what Nigerians can achieve when given the opportunity[44]. Philip Emeagwali

---

[43] www.math.buffalo.edu/mad/computer-science/emeagwali_philip.html

[44] Bill Clinton, *Remarks to a Joint Session of the Nigerian National Assembly in*

continues his work and research in the area of Mathematics and computing. He lives in the United States of America with his family.

3. Aliko Dangote

> *"I can remember when I was in primary school, I would go and buy cartons of sweets and I would start selling them just to make money. I was interested in business, even at that time.*[45]*"*

Aliko Dangote was born in 1957. He is the grandchild of one-time Africa's richest man – Sanusi Dantata. Dantata became wealthy from selling commodities like oats and rice. Dantata would eventually become Aliko Dangote's guardian, after his father died in 1965. By observing his grandfather's shrewdness and commitment to business, Aliko would quickly learn the rudiments of business and would be engaged in the enterprise right from his earliest childhood.

Aliko Dangote obtained a graduate degree from the Al-Azhar University when he was just 21 years old. A year later, 1977, Dangote approached his uncle for a loan of $3,000 to engage in a business opportunity he was convinced would be profitable. He was given the money and Dangote immediately imported some goods from Thailand and Brazil for sale in the Nigerian market. The business was so successful that he was able to return the initial capital to his uncle in three months.

This is the beginning of the Dangote business empire. Dangote would subsequently relocate to Lagos, where he has lived since, to run his business. Today, Dangote is involved in many business outlets such that his business empire is simply called the Dangote Group. The Dangote group includes Dangote Sugar refinery, Dangote Cement and Dangote Flour. Dangote Cement alone brings about 80% of the group's profit.

The Dangote Refinery, a multi-billion dollar outfit in Lekki Lagos, is almost nearing completion. Dangote Sugar is the main supplier of

---

Abuja, August 2000.
[45] www.allafrica.com/stories/201403240379.html

sugar to Nigeria's soft drink companies. They produce 800,000 tonnes of sugar annually. The Dangote group is the largest employer of labor in Nigeria after the Federal Government of Nigeria. Dangote Sugar alone employs 11,000 people. Aliko Dangote's net worth today is approximately $8.9 billion (US dollars).

Dangote, besides his entrepreneurial work, has also been involved in a lot of philanthropy. He is known to donate buildings to Nigerian tertiary institutions. He also donates generously to the ministry of sports in Nigeria. Aliko Dangote is a friend of politicians; although, so as not to court the wrong political enemies, he donates copiously to all leading political parties. When Muhammadu Buhari was announced winner of the Presidential elections in 2015, Dangote and some other prominent Nigerians were the first to visit him and felicitate with him.

Some have accused Dangote of enjoying favoritism from every government in power. While this may be so, one thing that cannot be taken away from him: Aliko Dangote has proven to be an astute businessman. He has shown that he can multiply whatever money that is put into his hands. For this reason, the country has benefited greatly from his business acumen and various business concerns. His employment of a large segment of Nigeria's unemployed youths still remains unrivaled in the history of the country. Recently, he brought out a scheme where drivers of his trucks must be graduates of tertiary institutions. Those employed under this scheme would enjoy so much leverage that would even include their possession of the very trucks that they drive, after a stipulated number of kilometers must have been covered by them. When the Nigerian government supports the Dangote business group to flourish, it is inadvertently supporting Nigerians themselves.

4. Hakeem Olajuwon

Hakeem Olajuwon was born in 1963 in Lagos, Nigeria, to Salim and Abike Olajuwon. Hakeem was raised in a strict Islamic home; a religion he still adheres to even in later life. He grew up like every other young Nigerian who loved to play football. Soon enough, Hakeem realized that his gifting was in goal-keeping. Hakeem's height and agility made him a good goal-keeper, although these qualities will later on serve him well in the field of basketball where he would go on to gain world renown. Hakeem was only introduced to basketball at the age of 17.

Hakeem Olajuwon, after a brief stint in Ahmadu Bello University in the early 1980s, moved to the United States of America for his tertiary education. While at the University of Houston, he was discovered by Coach Guy Lewis – who immediately recognized him as a player with talent in the game of basketball. Hakeem initially played college basketball. In 1984, he became the first overall selection in the 1984 NBA draft; a draft that included Michael Jordan, Charles Barkley and John Stockton.

Hakeem stands at a height of seven feet – a height that would stand him in advantage as he eventually became the number one center for the Houston Rockets. Hakeem Olajuwon led the Houston Rockets to the 1986 NBA finals, where they lost in six games to the Boston Celtics. He would however lead the same Rockets to win the NBA title back to back in the 1992 and 1993 seasons. In the 1993 season, Olajuwon became the only player in NBA history to win the NBA MVP, Defensive Player of the Year, and finals MVP. No other player has won all three honors in one season. Hakeem ended his career in 2002 with 3,830 points – which is 21.8 points per game, 13,747 rebounds – which translates to 11.1 rebounds per game, and 3,830 blocks – which means 3.1 blocks per game. Hakeem Olajuwon has been selected as one of the fifty greatest players in all of the history of the NBA.

In 2008, he was inducted into the Basketball Hall of Fame and in 2016 he was inducted into the FIBA Hall of Fame. Hakeem Olajuwon remains one of the greatest persons to have played the game of basketball in the United States of America. He owes his success to God's gracious providence, according to his Islamic beliefs, and to his early training in life where his parents inculcated in him a culture of hard work and discipline, and also in his seven other siblings. In retirement now, Hakeem spends his time between Jordan, where he has a home and where he moved to learn more on Islam; and his home in Houston, Texas, where he still trains young people in the rudiments of basketball. Unlike his colleagues, he has refused to take up a career in coaching. Rather he has chosen to invest in real estate in the United States of America where he earns a lot of money.

5. Linda Ikeji

In December 2018, Linda Ikeji introduced a new nomenclature to the world of internet blogging. Linda claimed she "fell pregnant" for a man whose identity she would not disclose immediately. The article was written as a kind of apology to her teeming fans whom she had always advocated feminine independency to. It was also a kind of disclaimer, where she sought to make it clear that although she would be having a child for this man, she intended to raise that child as a single parent. Her relationship with this man was over. This article, published on the popular Linda Ikeji blog, is what Linda Ikeja is typically known for: controversy. Linda Ikeji broke into the Nigerian scene as a popular blogger known for publishing controversial stories around celebrity figures. In the process, she had garnered quite a lot of followers and readers, she had made a name as a leading blogger in Nigeria, and she was also smiling to the bank in the process. Through blogging alone, Linda Ikeji has acquired a net worth of a little over a billion naira.

Linda Ikeji was born in 1980 to a middle class Roman Catholic family from Nkwerre, Imo State. At the age of 18, she was enrolled in the University of Lagos to study English language. To support herself in school and her family, Linda also worked as a waitress, a model and a writer while undergoing her undergraduate studies. With the coming of the internet, Linda Ikeji translated her love for writing to blogging. She founded the Linda Ikeji blog site, lindaikejisblog.com, in 2007 and has since become a household name in Nigeria in the process.

Because of the numerous controversial topics she has published on her site, Linda Ikeji has suffered a number of controversies. She has had clashes with the likes of Funke Akindele, Richard Mofe Damijo, Djimon Honsou, Wizkid and Tonto Dike. She has also made controversial publications on politicians like Doyin Okupe. On the 8th of October 2014, her blog site was shot down after it had been reported by an online user to Google. It would eventually be restored back two days later. But the momentary shutdown spurred Linda Ikeji to upgrade her website to be less dependent on Google.

In August 2012, Forbes Africa recognized Linda Ikeji as one of 20 prominent African women. In 2014, "Linda Ikeji" was the most searched item on Google search engines in Nigeria. In 2015, Linda Ikeji moved to her multi-million Naira mansion home in Lagos. She was interviewed in *Focus on Africa*, a BBC program, in September 2012.

In August 2018, Linda Ikeji received an honorary doctorate degree from Trinity International University in Georgia, USA, for her contribution to business and media in Africa. Linda Ikeji is a typical example of the can-do Nigerian spirit. Coming from a relatively poor background, grabbing an education and launching out into the adverse economic climate of Nigeria, Linda Ikeji waded her way into success. She never flinches from the idea that she is self-made. Although she can be quite ostentatious in her manner of outing, she would be the first to claim that a person who has worked hard is entitled to luxury and whatever self-adulation they choose to confer on themselves.

6. Ngozi Okonjo-Iweala

When Olusegun Obasano assumed power in 1999, he came face to face with a debt profile of $30 billion from a group called the Paris Club. A little investigation into the profile of these debts showed that much of the money had been spent on non-existent projects by previous military administrations. Obasanjo spent a lot of time during his first term to obtain debt relief. When he could not get it, during his second term in office, he sought the help of Ngozi Okonjo-Iweala, who was at that time working at the World Bank in Washington D.C, U.S.A. Obasanjo writes:

> *"After my first term, I realized that my talks at the highest levels needed follow-up at the levels below. So, I head-hunted Ngozi Okonjo-Iweala from the World Bank, appointing her as Nigeria's Finance Minister.[46]"*

Before the end of Obasanjo tenure, the Nigerian debt profile had been reduced from $30 billion to $12 billion. This sum was quickly paid by the Nigerian government and the country was rid of a debilitating debt

---

[46] Olawoyin, Oladeinde. Why I head-hunted Okonjo-Iweala to become finance minister – Obasanjo. Premium Times. August 14th, 2017. Accessed: December 27th, 2019. www.premiumtimeng.com/news/headlines/240147-why-i-head-hunted-okonjo-iweala-to-become-finance-minister-obasanjo.html

profile that the country had been using $3 billion annually to service. This great feat was accomplished by Ngozi Okonjo-Iweala. It immediately brought her name into prominence in Nigeria.

Ngozi Okonjo-Iweala was born in June 1954 to the family of Professor Chukwuka Okonjo at the University of Ibadan. She had her early education in International School, Ibadan, and St. Anne's School, Molete, Ibadan. She would eventually bag a degree in Economics from Harvard University. Ngozi Okonjo-Iweala spent 25 years working at the World Bank in Washington D.C, where she rose to the number 2 position as a Managing Director.

In 2003, she was appointed Nigeria's Finance Minister by President Olusegun Obasanjo. She would later return as Finance Minister under President Goodluck Jonathan. She would be remembered for her efforts in reducing Nigeria's Paris Club debt profile. She also introduced the concept of an "Excess Crude Account" that was used to shore up the country's external financial reserves. She introduced the idea of publishing each state of the federation's monthly financial allocations.

This action brought transparency to the finances of states in the country and reduced the pillaging of state funds by unscrupulous state governors. She introduced the concept of Treasury Single Account (TSA), which the Buhari government is using to curb corruption among public institutions. Okonjo-Iweala also brought about the Integrated Payroll and Personal Information System (IPPIS), which has helped curb corruption in the federal government's payroll system.

Many people do not like Ngozi Okonjo-Iweala because she brought much transparency to our national life. People would rather that the country continues in darkness so that corruption may continue unabated. For this, she was eventually frustrated from the Obasanjo's government in 2007. In recent times, her name has been included to be running mate to leading political figures. While she has returned to her World Bank job as a consultant, Ngozi Okonjo-Iweala still looks on her beloved Nigeria with the hope that she can serve her better in the future.

7. Davido

Davido is the new face of entertainment in Nigeria and Africa in general. With his genre of music "afro-hip hop", Davido has proven to the world that music is innate in Nigeria and thus continue to lift the flag of entertainment for the country around the world. Davido likes to call himself "Omo Baba Olowo", which is also the title of his first studio album. *Omo Baba Olowo* means the child of a wealthy man.

Davido was born David Adedeji Adeleke in November 1992, to a business magnate, Chief Adedeji Adeleke. The older Adeleke is the owner of Adeleke University in Ede, Osun State, and he is also the chairman of many business concerns all around Nigeria. Unlike his father, Davido took to music early in life. While studying Business Administration at Oakwood University, USA, Davido dropped out to pursue a career in music.

First, he began by making beats recording and would eventually go on to record his own songs. His first single "Dami Duro" was an instant hit. It would feature prominently in his first studio album, "Omo Baba Olowo" in 2012. By the year 2015, Davido had released other singles like "Gobe", "One of a Kind", "Skelewu", "Aye", and a lot of others. In 2017, Davido released "If" and "Fall", the two tracks are about his most successful and most listened to songs since his music career began. "If" generated much reaction on social media, while "Fall" become the longest charting Nigerian song on the Billboard charts.

Despite Davido's successes, his life has also been laced with a string of controversies. In December 2015, Davido fell into a custody drama with one of his "baby mamas", Sophia Momodu, after the latter accused him of wanting to illegally traffic their child out of Nigeria without her permission. The matter was subsequently settled amicably between the two former lovers.

In October 2017, one of Davido's friends, Tagbo, was found dead in controversial circumstances. Tagbo, Davido and some other friends had been out drinking. Tagbo may have fallen into a drunken fit but the friends who were unaware of his peculiar medical condition, left him in the car and went away to a shop to buy things. By the time they would return, Tagbo was already gasping for breath. He would eventually be taken to a hospital where he was pronounced dead.

Davido claimed he knew nothing about the death, while Tagbo's family accused him of not taking care of his friend who was in his custody. The matter would eventually be taken out of the media glare after the Lagos State Police intervened.

In spite of his controversial way of life, Davido remains one of the leading entertainment figures in Nigeria's music industry. His presence draws thousands to events. He is the most followed Nigerian on Instagram and he continues to ride high on his celebrity status around the country.

8. Chimamanda Adichie

Some have touted Chimamanda Adichie as the one to succeed the Nigerian Nobel Laureate, Professor Wole Soyinka, in the world of Nigerian literature. She has indeed risen to such a height as to compete with the best writers in the world. A Nobel Laureate will be a fitting way to bring her illustrious writing career to a head.

While Chimamanda was born in 1977, her life pursuit would eventually be propelled by a family tragedy: both her grandfathers had been tragically killed in the Nigerian Civil War that started exactly a decade before she was born. The young Adichie family had lost everything to the war and had to begin to rebuild. It was in the middle of this rebuilding that Chimamanda was born. Her father, James Nwoye Adichie, was a Professor of Statistics with the University of Nigeria, Nsukka(UNN).

Her mother, Grace Ifeoma, was the first female registrar of the same University. Chimamanda grew up in this middle class family and would go on to study Medicine and Pharmacy at UNN. It was not long before she discovered that she was not cut out for the medical field. She dropped out of this discipline after eighteen months, and left Nigeria to study communication and political science in the USA. In 2003, she completed a Master Degree in Creative Writing from John Hopkins University.

Chimamanda Adichie's first book was *Purple Hibiscus* published in 2003. She wrote *Half of a Yellow Sun* in 2006, and something close to a Memoir, *Americanah,* in 2013. Her short stories collections, *The Thing*

Around Your Neck, was published in 2009. She has written other notable books since she emerged in the literary scene in 2003.

Adichie's book, *Purple Hibiscus*, received international acclaim. It was awarded the Commonwealth Writers Prize for Best First Book in 2005. "Half of a Yellow Sun" a book that depicts life in war-torn Igbo land during the Nigerian civil war, won the Orange Prize for Fiction in 2007. The book has since been adapted to a film directed by Biyi Bandele. Her book "Americanah" was selected by the New York Times as one of the ten best books of 2013. Her latest book, "A Feminist's Manifesto in Fifteen Suggestions", is a book she wrote portraying her beliefs in feminism and certain advises she gives on how to raise young girls to be feminists.

Chimamanda Adichie spends her time writing, and travelling between Nigeria and the United States, teaching creative writing. She is married to Ivara Esege.

9. Bennet Omalu

The movie "Concussion" is about a black forensic pathologist who had the nerve to suggest to the American football league, the NFL, that players were likely to develop a brain condition that would affect their lives adversely in the future as a result of the games they play.

He suggested that the constant trauma to the head that the game of football was bringing on players, had a high percentage likelihood of developing into a condition he called Chronic Traumatic Encephalopathy (CTE), which in natural parlance is called a "concussion". The suggestion was radical and had the potential of affecting the multi-billion dollar American football business. This doctor is Bennet Omalu and he is a Nigerian.

Bennet Omalu was born in September 1968 in Anambra, Nigeria, in the heat of the Nigerian civil war. He is the sixth of the family's eight children. His family had to flee their home after his birth and would only return two years after, following the end of the war. Omalu attended the Federal Government College, Enugu, and went to the University of Nsukka (UNN) for his bachelor degree in medicine and surgery. Omalu left Nigeria in the heat of the June 12, 1993 crisis, and went to Washington in 1993 to complete a fellowship at the University of Washington. Omalu would eventually train to be a neuropathologist. He also holds seven other advanced degrees.

In 2002, Bennet Omalu performed autopsy on a former Pittsburgh Steelers player, Mike Webster, and this led to a re-emergence of awareness on a neurologic condition with chronic head trauma. This condition was previously found in boxers and some other professional athletes.

Omalu's finding suggested that this condition was also likely to be prevalent among American Footballers. He would later publish his findings in the Journal of Neurosurgery in 2005 in a paper titled "Chronic Traumatic Encephalopathy in a National Football League Player". In it Omalu called for further studies on the condition. In 2006, Omalu published another paper based on his pathological work on the brain of Terry Long, another former American Football player who had committed suicide in 2005. By this time, Omalu was beginning to draw the conclusions that there was a strong link between CTE, suicide and the American football players. He presented his finding to the boards of the NFL but they dismissed his findings.

However, in March 2016, the NFL Senior Vice President for Health and Safety matters, Jeff Miller, testified before the American Congress saying that the NFL now acknowledged that there is a strong link between football and CTE. This acknowledgement means that the NFL can now take more safety precautions for their players who are involved in these games.

Bennet Omalu continues to practice medicine in the United States. He is a Professor at the Department of Medical Pathology and Laboratory Science at the University of California. He is married to Prema Mutiso, a Kenyan, and they have two children: Ashly and Mark. Bennet Omalu became a United States citizen in February 2015. His work as a pathologist has however changed the way and manner the game of NFL is played in the United States of America today.

10. Genevieve Nnanji

While Nigerian movies have become quite popular worldwide, especially around Africa, the usual criticism of our films is that they do not have quality. That our movie makers spend more time producing works of quantity and not quality. Genevieve Nnanji was on a quest to change all of that narrative when she produced the movie "Lionheart" – a movie she directed herself.

It was a movie that was produced to be shown on NETFLIX, an online movie streaming network. The quality of "Lionheart" would however be acknowledged when earlier this year, the prestigious American movie awards, the Academy Awards a.k.a the Oscars, received "Lionheart" under the category of foreign films. The news of the first Nigerian film to be received into the Oscars was greeted with much celebrations by Nigerians.

However, in November, the Academy Awards committee disqualified "Lionheart" from the foreign film category. They said that a film under the category of foreign film is expected to have been made with a foreign language spoken. Of the 95 minutes duration of Lionheart, only 11 minutes was Igbo. So it failed to meet up with the standard for a foreign film. Many people protested the Academy Awards, saying that Nigeria's lingua franca was English. But this fell on deaf ears. Nevertheless, Nigerians can claim that one of their own had made a movie that met true international standards for it to have been received for consideration by the Academy Awards.

Genevieve Nnaji was born in Imo State in 1979 and was raised in Lagos. She studied Creative Arts at the University of Lagos but had been acting even before she went to the university. She was a child actor who had appeared in a sitcom called "Ripples" at the age of eight. Genevieve first film role was in "Most Wanted" in 1998. She was only 19. In 2010, she did "Ije: The Journey". So far she has starred in no less than 200 films.

In 2005, she won the African Movie Academy Award for Best Actress. In 2003, she was awarded the best actress by the Censors Board of Nigeria. In 2009, Oprah Winfrey called her the "Julia Roberts" of African movies. In November 2015, Nnaji produced her first movie "Road to Yesterday". She made her directorial debut in September 2018 with "Lionheart". The movie was acquired by Netflix, making it the first movie by Netflix originally from Nigeria. Netflix purchased the movie for a whopping $3.8 million (N1.39 Billion) – making Genevieve the first billionaire movie maker in Nigeria.

Nigeria's Human Resources

When the central problem of Nigeria is to be analyzed by some, they say that our problem is one of leadership. The great Nigerian novelist, Chinua Achebe, once said that the singular problem of Nigeria is that of bad leadership. Others say that the problem of Nigeria is corruption, especially as seen in the squandering of the nation's resources. They take this claim from the fact that Nigeria is an oil producing country and thus its people have no business being poor. They aver that if the resources of the country are better utilized, everyone should be able to have a bit of the national cake.

This writer, however, is of the opinion that Nigerian foremost problem is its underutilization of her human resources. Nigeria is the largest Black Country in the world. It is the most populated in Africa with 200 million people, only followed by Egypt in a distant position with 80 million people. This country has more than enough persons who can lead the nation to Eldorado. We have gifted individuals in every sphere of life.

The nation, divided into six geo-political zones, has every part of it that is rich in some aspect of human life that can benefit the whole country. Northern Nigeria has always been known for its vast land mass and their availability for agriculture. Eastern Nigerians are known for their industry, entrepreneurship, and inventions. Western Nigerians are known for the mental acumen and advancement in education.

The South-South of the country is rich in petroleum deposits. The middle belt is rich in natural resources like gold, tin and so on. What this country needs are people who can be better galvanized to use the resources of the country to make the nation move forward.

It was the Ghanaian writer, Ayi Kwei Armah, that wrote the book "The Beautiful Ones Are Not Yet Born". He wrote it with obvious reference to the fact that those who would save a certain nationality from doom are yet to come forth. In Nigeria, the beautiful ones are here. This chapter has purposely listed ten Nigerians that have excelled in various fields.

The list can be extended to thousands of other Nigerians but there is really no space for such in a chapter like this. Nigerians, despite the harsh economic realities and bad leadership they have had to endure, have continued to thrive in their various fields of endeavors. The Nigerian genius is further amplified when Nigerians get to the diaspora and can enjoy those incentives that would make one's work thrive.

They simply excel. This is the story of many of the people listed in the ten above and this is how the country will be saved in the days to come. Nigerians within the country will begin to salvage the nation when we realize that no one else will do it for us. At the same time, Nigerians in the diaspora, whose every waking moment is used to think about their fatherland, will also begin to send resources and man-power to help the country. This writer envisions that it is the good people of Nigeria, these great Nigerians that would stand up and save the country. As this happens, some of us who are writers will be around to document these progress. We would be looking at a nation move from decline to rise to its inherent potentials. This will be our story; this would be our song.

THE END!!!